TELL THE WHOLE WORLD TO SING A NEW SONG TO THE LORD!
TELL THOSE WHO SAIL THE OCEAN AND THOSE WHO LIVE FAR AWAY
TO JOIN IN THE PRAISE.
Isaiah 42:10

ALSO BY ROBIN DALE MATTISON

A companion journal to *WaterWords*,
T.R.U.E. NORTH: Steering by Scripture at Sea,
Published by Maritime Library.
Visit waterwords.net or contact info@waterwords.net.

WATER WORDS

COVER ART

The original painting used on the cover of this book was created by YONG XIAN-RANG, former Head of Folk Art Department at the Central Academy of Art in Beijing. Internationally known for his techniques, Professor Yong Xian-rang's works of art are treasured in collections in Britain, Japan, France, Korea, Taiwan and the United States. The art reproduced on the cover is dedicated to all the *People of the Sea*. For more information on his art, contact info@waterwords.net.

SEA READINGS FOR THE PEOPLE OF THE SEA

Robin Dale Mattison

MALL PUBLISHING, INC.

BEACH PARK, IL USA

Published in 2003 by
Maritime Library
Mall Publishing, Inc.
10240 W. Ames Avenue
Beach Park IL 60099 USA

Cover Art: Yong Xian-rang
Book Design: Maritime Library, Mall Publishing, Inc.

Queries regarding rights and permissions should be addressed to the publisher

ISBN 0-9673673-4-4 (softcover)
ISBN 0-9673673-3-6 (hardcover)

PHOTO CREDITS
Barbara Anderson, Allen Butte, Thomas Callahan, George Davis, Andrew Krey, Ted Mall,
Robin Mattison, Judie Schwalm, National Aeronautics and Space Administration,
National Oceanic and Atmospheric Administration, George True, Jean van Hemert.

CONTACT
For licensing/copyright information, or for additional copies of this book, write to:
MARITIME LIBRARY
10240 W. Ames Av., Beach Park IL 60099
e-mail: info@waterwords.net
Web Site: www.mallpublishing.net

For
All the People of the Sea

Dedication

The Rev. Ray Eckhoff
Maritime Chaplain
1930–2000

This volume is dedicated to our dear Christian friend and brother Chaplain, the Rev. Ray Eckhoff, who began a Seafarers Bible Correspondence Course out of his maritime chaplaincy in Tacoma, Washington in 1977. We give thanks to God for his ministry. We are humbled by his willingness to trust the further development of the Seafarers' Bible Correspondence Course to the Lutheran Association for Maritime Ministry. We only wish he could have been here to teach it to seafarers with us. Yet, as he would have said, *To God be the glory!*

Table of Contents

Acknowledgments

The Lutheran Association for Maritime Ministry (LAMM) is deeply grateful to the Aid Association for Lutherans (now known as Thrivent Financial for Lutherans) for a start-up grant for the creation and publication of this book of sea readings for seafarers. Their interest and patience with this valuable mission project is greatly appreciated.

We give thanks to God for:
The Rev. Dr. Robin D. Mattison, Associate Professor of New Testament and Greek at the Lutheran Theological Seminary at Philadelphia, PA., for developing, writing and editing this volume.

Chaplain Andrew Krey, Executive Secretary, LAMM as well as Ruth K. Stark, Shirley A. Dickau, and the LAMM Board of Directors for their oversight of this project and their commitment to its continuance.

Glenn L. Simmons and Iris Frick for their input and assistance in proof reading.

Foreword

Dear People of the Sea,

May the grace and peace of God be with you as you sail the oceans. We thank God for your vocation on the sea and your bringing us on land so many varied cargoes. By your hard and heartfelt labor you supply many needed products.

We know, as maritime chaplains and maritime missionaries, that the Bible has much to say to you as a modern seafarer or fisher. The Bible witnesses to what you already know. Water is both a blessing and a danger to people, especially to those who make their living on the sea.

We have developed *WaterWords* to fulfil a long-felt need for a comprehensive biblical resource for the people of the sea. This is it! *WaterWords* is specially designed for seafarers with a selection of biblical texts for study, meditation and for reading out loud in worship. It contains a full collection of the rich stories, psalms (songs), laws and letters from the Bible that relate to a working life on the powerful sea. We know your seafaring life is marked by long distances and long times away from family. We know you labor hard and serve among crews of many nations amidst the great dangers and the great beauty of the sea. *WaterWords* will tell you how much God cares for you in the midst of all that may happen in your life at sea.

WaterWords is the first book in a multi-volume publishing venture. We have focused this volume and its companion journal, *T.R.U.E. NORTH: Steering by Scripture at Sea,* on readings from the Bible about the sea and seafaring. If you read through *WaterWords* from beginning to end, it will be clear that God continually acts to save people from the sea, from themselves and from those evils that oppress them. In this way, this first volume is a sea-salvation history for those new to the love of God in Jesus Christ. The next volumes will be on the Gospel of John and the Epistle of Paul to the Romans. A book on living the life of faith as a Christian at sea and other volumes on books of the New and Old Testaments will follow.

If you are already a believing seafarer, you will find this volume designed to strengthen your faith as you read more of Scripture and God's will for your life. Be assured that this volume is intentionally written to be an aid for the faith development of any Christian. Since its major content is Scripture, it can be used without worry by any seafarer, including chaplains, ship's visitors, and ministering seafarers. In this project, we are committed to providing quality resources for all individuals, denominations and church ministries proclaiming the love of God in Christ.

There is much more that God wants to say to you through Scripture than just these watery images, but these readings are a good place to start! We hope that you will keep *WaterWords* next to your Bible. If you don't yet have a Bible, ask a chaplain or ship's visitor for one; or let us know you need one by writing to the address below and tell us which language you prefer to read. We have some bilingual Bibles in English and another language, such as Chinese. We want to help you if possible.

You may want to read *WaterWords* in the privacy of your cabin. We would also encourage you to find other seafarers with whom to study. If you would like a Christian on shore with whom you could discuss what you are reading or your written reflections from the journal *T.R.U.E. NORTH*, please write to us at the address at the bottom of this letter. We will locate a Bible pen pal for you. This Christian will pray for you daily in light of your exchange of letters. We trust that you will pray for them too! There is more detail about having a Bible pen pal in *T.R.U.E. NORTH: Steering by Scripture at Sea*, a companion journal to this volume.

We pray that we may continue to be your servants because of the wondrous love the God of the sea and of seafarers has shown through Jesus Christ. This Jesus calmed the waves, rescued the drowning, and turned water into wine. In Jesus Christ, God's own Son, we have found meaning, comfort and joy for ourselves when we are in difficulty. Jesus will do the same for you.

God loves you!

The Rev. Dr. Bill Hempel, Chaplain
President, Lutheran Association for Maritime Ministry

The Rev. Andrew Krey, Chaplain
Executive Secretary, Lutheran Association for Maritime Ministry

Seafarers' Bible Correspondence Course
P.O. Box 786, Charlestown Beach, RI 02813 USA
www.waterwords.net, e-mail: info@waterwords.net

Introduction

Welcome aboard! We have included in *WaterWords* all the important biblical readings referring to the seas, oceans, rivers or water in the Bible. There are many sea readings and they have much to teach. Below is an overview of where this study voyage will take you.

The Sea in the Old Testament

Many biblical passages in the Old Testament describe how God is connected to the wonder and dangers of rivers and oceans, rain and thunderstorms. In Genesis, the first book of the Bible, God settled and separated the raging waters from 'below the sky' from the waters 'above the sky', so that there might be dry land on which people could live (Genesis 1.6-10). On that dry land, God channeled the waters into rivers so that people might drink freely and safely (Genesis 2.10-14).

Believers also wrote about how God's own purpose controlled rivers and oceans. Believers wrote how God caused the Red Sea to part so God's people could cross the seabed on dry ground (Exodus 14.1-15.21). A hymn writer sang that the oceans roared and the rivers clapped their hands in praise to God (Psalm. 98.8). One prophet, a messenger of God, described God's words as like fresh water on the earth (Isaiah 55.10-11). The prophet Ezekiel reported the destruction of evil seafaring nations that defied God and harmed the faithful and many other nations (Ezekiel 27.1-36).

People of the Sea and the People of God

Some of these writers must have been seafarers and fishers, since they told two very important sea stories. One was about God's Chief Mate, Noah, who survived the great flood (Genesis 6.5-9.17). The other was about Jonah, the reluctant, seagoing prophet, who was shocked to end up for a time in the belly of God's great fish, Leviathan (Jonah 1.1-4.11).

The Sea in the New Testament

In the New Testament, Jesus showed he was the Son of God when he controlled a storm at sea and rescued his disciple shipmates (Matthew 8.18-27). He changed water into wine, taking something necessary for survival (water) and making it into something of delight and joy (wine) (John 2.1-12). He continually ministered to fishers along the Sea of Galilee and told parables about fishing (Matthew 13.47-50). He said that obeying his words would make his seafaring hearers safe from floods of evil (Matthew 7.24-29). Jesus talked about the seafarers Noah and Jonah in relation to his own ministry (Luke 3.23-27; 11:29-32 and their parallels in Matthew and Mark). Jesus chose baptism, a washing in water under the power of God's word of blessing, as the sign of God's commitment to people (Matthew 28.18-20). It became the entrance ritual of the Christian community and was written about many times in the New Testament. Jesus' followers were promised that God's refreshing water would well up in them for eternal life (John. 4.14).

People of the Sea and Apostles for Jesus Christ
Several of the first apostles, Simon Peter, Andrew, James and John were fishers (Mark 1.16-20). Peter followed Jesus and became the first ministering fisher for Christ. Another, Paul of Tarsus, ended up as a skilled seafarer because he was so often onboard ship carrying out God's mission. He was shipwrecked three times (2 Corinthians 11.25)! Still, Paul continued to sail the Mediterranean Sea to spread the Gospel from Asia Minor to Spain. He became a chaplain to seafarers on one of those voyages (Acts 27.1-28.16).

Prophecies of God's Eternal Reign Involving the Sea
Isaiah, Jeremiah and Ezekiel had confidence that God's eternal reign would be marked by the end of the dangerous salt waters described in Genesis 1.1-28. The prophet Daniel interpreted dreams of God conquering the dangerous beasts that arose from the sea at the end times (Daniel 7.1-14). In the last book of the Bible, Revelation, John of Patmos prophesied that the sea would give up its dead at the end of time. Believers would then find themselves gathered around the throne of God, standing on a sea that has become solid like glass. They would be sustained by the sweet fresh stream of water that would flow from the throne of God (Revelation 21.1-8). This fresh water first flowed in Genesis in the rivers that God created in the Garden of Eden. So, at the end of time, God will reaffirm God's ordering of the waters at the creation and then will offer a new ordering of the waters that will quench thirst for all time.

The Plan of the Entries in the Volume
We have chosen one hundred and twelve (114) sea readings in *Water Words*. They are equally divided between the Old and the New Testament. Overall, there are selections from thirty-four of the sixty-six books of the Bible plus

one from the Old Testament Apocrypha. The Apocrypha is a collection of other writings from the time of the Old Testament written by believers.

The order of entries in any section of *WaterWords* follows that of the Bible. Sometimes a passage involving the sea or fresh water is recorded in the Bible in more than one place. This happens especially in the stories of Jesus' water wonders in the New Testament. We have made only one entry where there are doublets and triplets. We will note the other locations of such passages so you might look them up in your own Bible.

True North: Reflections for Your Response

Before each reading, there will be a title that describes the content of the selection. Following each title we have written a few sentences titled, *True North*. These are there to help you see how these readings about God are also commenting on your life with God. Each *True North* reflection gives you a chance to think about your relationship to God in light of the passage that will follow. In a general way, each passage focuses on one of these matters: 1) God's relationship to you, 2) the help God gives believers, 3) the witness of seafarers to God, 4) the life, death and resurrection of Jesus, 5) Baptism and Holy Communion which are the rituals by which Christians come together by command of our Lord Jesus, 6) the witnesses to God's action against chaos in the present and at the end of time and 7) your response to God. We designed these reflections to provide you with words of hope, courage, forgiveness and blessing in the midst of the difficult seafaring life.

T.R.U.E. NORTH: Steering by Scripture at Sea

The brief meditations that we have provided are just a starting point for your meditating and praying. Your personal understanding of the passages is even more important than what we have offered. We would be remiss if we didn't help you to study Scripture by yourself when the chaplains have gone ashore.

We have developed in a companion journal to *WaterWords* a four-step plan for you to study these passages for yourself and write about them. In the introduction to that volume we will teach you that plan, which uses the word *T.R.U.E.* as a memory aid. The four steps are: 1) Turn to God's Word for Safe Passage, 2) Read Yourself into God's WaterWords, 3) Unite with God's through Prayer, and 4) Embark with God on this Day's Voyage of Faith. We call the overall journal *T.R.U.E. NORTH: Steering by Scripture at Sea*. In the next section you will see an outline of this plan, but the details are in the accompanying journal. You may want to read the introduction to that journal first so that you can learn the procedure or you may want to simply start on your own.

You may use the spaces in the journal to respond to the reflections we have written in *WaterWords* or to work in greater detail on the four-step plan, *T.R.U.E. North*. You may need much more space to write your reflections than what we have given you. A plain piece of paper will work just as well. We encourage you to use *WaterWords* and the journal *T.R.U.E. NORTH* in any way that is useful to you.

If you do not have the *T.R.U.E. NORTH* journal or need additional copies, write to: Seafarers Bible Correspondence Course, P.O. Box 786, Charlestown Beach, RI 02813 USA. You may e-mail info@waterwords.net or visit www.waterwords.net. However, it is not necessary to have the journal to gain spiritual refreshment from *WaterWords*.

A Note to Chaplains, Ship's Visitors and Ministering Seafarers

You can use any of the volumes in *WaterWords* in a number of ways. They may be a resource for learning about the Bible and the basics of the Christian faith, for private study and meditation, for small group discussion or as readings for worship. In addition, we are committed to providing the land-based support for these volumes to be a Seafarers' Bible Correspondence Course. In each volume will be questions and opportunities for reflection to aid in faith development. These can be sent to shore by way of the post, a chaplain or a ship's visitor to the Seafarers' Christian Fellowship at the address in the box above. Then, a Bible pen pal will be assigned to respond to seafarers' concerns, be they spiritual, familial or practical. Our goal is to make use of the faithful insights of believers on shore in congregations as an extension of the meaningful but often fleeting relationships between seafarers and chaplains and other ship's visitors. We pray that our endeavor will be a blessing to you in your important and faithful ministry.

Robin Dale Mattison

T.R.U.E. North: Steering by Scripture at Sea
A Summary of the Four-Step Plan

Step 1

T **Turn to God's Word for Safe Passages**
Trust God
Tell God about Yourself
Thank God

Step 2

R **Read Yourself into God's Water Words**
Read Yourself into God's Story in <u>this</u> Passage
How did God or Jesus act toward the sea and the people in this passage?
How did evil affect the sea and the people in this passage?
How did God or Jesus bring blessing out of this evil?
How did people respond to being blessed in the present or saved for eternal life?
How did religious authorities and religious leaders help people to trust God?

Read God's Story into Your Life at Sea from this passage
How is God or Jesus acting toward you, your shipmates and family in a similar way?
How is evil affecting you, your shipmates and family?
How is God or Jesus bringing blessing out of evil for you, your shipmates and family?
How are you, your shipmates and family responding to being blessed in the present or saved for eternal life?
How are religious authorities and religious readers helping you, your shipmates and family to trust God or Jesus in a similar way?

Respond to the True North Reflections in WaterWords
Read Your Own Name into God's Word

Step 3

U Unite with God through Prayer
Praise God's Eternal Glory and Power
Ask God for Forgiveness for Your Sins
Thank God for God's Word, Daily Blessings and Eternal Life
Pray that You, Your Shipmates and Family Might be Saved from Evil

Step 4

E Embark with God on This Day's Voyage of Faith
Enjoy the Sea
Ease the life and death of the creatures of the water
Esteem all of God's creation including your shipmates
Encourage care for the fragile sea environment
Empower Your Voyage with God's Word
Enlighten your day with a memory verse or phrase
Extend to yourself a message of hope
Expect the Holy Spirit to empower and sustain you
Energize your seafaring life with shipboard worship
Encircle your ship with prayer for its crew and its captain
Encourage One Another
Enhance life on board by doing good for a shipmate
Exchange hatred for love
Explain the Christian hope you have within you
E-mail your family

Books of the Bible and their Abbreviations Cited in WaterWords
According to the Contemporary English Version

The Old Testament
God's Witness to and through Israel to the Nations

The Torah (Law and teachings):
Genesis (Gn)
Exodus (Ex)
Leviticus (Le)
Numbers (Nu)
Deuteronomy (Dt)

The Historical Books:
2 Samuel (2 S)
2 Kings (2 K)

The Poetic or Wisdom Books:
Job (Job)
Psalms (Ps)
Proverbs (Pr)
Ecclesiastes (Ec)
Song of Songs (Sgs)

The Major Prophets:
Isaiah (Is)
Jeremiah (Jr)
Ezekiel (Ez)

The Minor Prophets:
Amos (Am)
Jonah (Jon)
Micah
Daniel (Dn)
Habakkuk (Hb)

The Old Testament Apocrypha
The Wisdom of Solomon

The New Testament
Jesus Christ's Witness to God and through Israel to the Nations

The Four Gospels:
Matthew (Mt)
Mark (Mk)
Luke (Lk)
John (Jn)

The Acts of the Apostles:
Acts (Ac)

The Letters of the Apostle Paul and His Followers to Gentile (formerly pagan) Christians:
Romans (Ro)
1 Corinthians (1 Co)

2 Corinthians (2 Co)
Galatians (Ga)
1 Thessalonians (1 Th)
Titus (Titus)

Letters and Writings of Jewish Christians to Jewish-Christians who believed in Israel's God and in Christ:
Hebrews (He)
James (Jas)
1 Peter (1 P)
The Revelation of John (Rev)

How God Began Creation by Making Order of the Roaring Waters

Genesis 1.1-31, 2.1-4a
God Separated the Waters Above the Earth (Fresh Waters)
From the Waters Below the Earth (Salt Waters)

*True North: God loved you enough to create a world in which to delight
and rejoice in God and other creatures. Did you know your seafaring life was
dependent on God making the seas safer for your labor and your travel?*

¹ In the beginning God
    created the heavens
        and the earth.
²   The earth was barren,
        with no form of life;
    it was under a roaring ocean
        covered with darkness.
    But the Spirit of God
        was moving over the water.

The First Day
    ³ God said, "I command light to shine!" And light started
shining. ⁴ God looked at the light and saw that it was good. He separated
light from darkness ⁵ and named the light "Day" and the darkness
"Night." Evening came and then morning—that was the first day.

The Second Day
⁶ God said, "I command a dome to separate the water above it from
the water below it." ⁷ And that's what happened. God made the dome

[8] and named it "Sky." Evening came and then morning—that was the second day.

The Third Day

[9] God said, "I command the water under the sky to come together in one place, so there will be dry ground." And that's what happened. [10] God named the dry ground "Land," and he named the water "Ocean." God looked at what he had done and saw that it was good.
[11] God said, "I command the earth to produce all kinds of plants, including fruit trees and grain." And that's what happened. [12] The earth produced all kinds of vegetation. God looked at what he had done, and it was good. [13] Evening came and then morning—that was the third day.

The Fourth Day

[14] God said, "I command lights to appear in the sky and to separate day from night and to show the time for seasons, special days, and years. [15] I command them to shine on the earth." And that's what happened. [16] God made two powerful lights, the brighter one to rule the day and the other to rule the night. He also made the stars. [17] Then God put these lights in the sky to shine on the earth, [18] to rule day and night, and to separate light from darkness. God looked at what he had done, and it was good. [19] Evening came and then morning—that was the fourth day.

The Fifth Day

[20] God said, "I command the ocean to be full of living creatures, and I command birds to fly above the earth." [21] So God made the giant sea monsters and all the living creatures that swim in the ocean. He also made every kind of bird. God looked at what he had done, and it was good. [22] Then he gave the living creatures his blessing—he told the ocean creatures to live everywhere in the ocean and the birds to live everywhere on earth. [23] Evening came and then morning—that was the fifth day.

The Sixth Day

[24] God said, "I command the earth to give life to all kinds of tame animals, wild animals, and reptiles." And that's what happened. [25] God made every one of them. Then he looked at what he had done, and it was good.

[26] God said, "Now we will make humans, and they will be like us. We will let them rule the fish, the birds, and all other living creatures." [27] So God created humans to be like himself; he made men and women. [28] God gave them his blessing and said:

Have a lot of children! Fill the earth with people and bring it under your control. Rule over the fish in the ocean, the birds in the sky, and every animal on the earth. [29] I have provided all kinds of fruit and grain for you to eat. [30] And I have given the green plants as food for everything else that breathes. These will be food for animals, both wild and tame, and for birds.

[31] God looked at what he had done. All of it was very good! Evening came and then morning—that was the sixth day.

2.[1] So the heavens and the earth and everything else were created.

The Seventh Day

[2] By the seventh day God had finished his work, and so he rested. [3] God blessed the seventh day and made it special because on that day he rested from his work.

[4] That's how God created the heavens and the earth.

Genesis 2.4a-14
God Caused A River To Flow
From the Garden of Eden to Water the World

True North: From the beginning of time to the end of time, God provides the sweet water you need to live. A river of sweet water will still flow from the throne of God at the end of time. You'll find this promise at Revelation 22.1-3 in the last section of WaterWords.

[4] When the Lord God made the heavens and the earth, [5] no grass or plants were growing anywhere. God had not yet sent any rain, and there was no one to work the land. [6] But streams came up from the ground and watered the earth.

[7] The Lord God took a handful of soil and made a man. God breathed life into the man, and the man started breathing. [8] The Lord

made a garden in a place called Eden, which was in the east, and he put the man there.

[9] The Lord God placed all kinds of beautiful trees and fruit trees in the garden. Two other trees were in the middle of the garden. One of the trees gave life—the other gave the power to know the difference between right and wrong.

[10] From Eden a river flowed out to water the garden, then it divided into four rivers. [11] The first one is the Pishon River that flows through the land of Havilah, [12] where pure gold, rare perfumes, and precious stones are found. [13] The second is the Gihon River that winds through Ethiopia. [14] The Tigris River that flows east of Assyria is the third, and the fourth is the Euphrates River.

Genesis 3.1-24
The Waters are Ordered but People are Not!

True North: It took two people for God to get forgotten! The first married couple lived an eternal life in the fruitful Garden of Eden by the ever-flowing sweet waters. Then they decided to believe a snake! They were bit by the desire to know as much as God did. Therefore, God kept Adam and Eve away from the tree of eternal life that grew out of the fresh sweet waters in the garden. The earth also was cursed by their disobedience. Henceforth, everything would die. Adam and Eve would sweat for their food. Water would not always be safe, sweet or plentiful. Sadly, knowing as much as God did didn't work as well as trusting God's word! Now they had knowledge but no safety! Still, God did not abandon Adam and Eve, or us, their children, to eternal guilt and shame. God has kept on talking to us, calling us back, providing for us and making justice for all people, even while being grieved by our disobedience. Yet, God has promised through many prophets that those fresh sweet waters and the tree of life will flourish again for all creation the kingdom of God. Read Revelation 22.1-17.

3 The snake was sneakier than any of the other wild animals that the LORD God had made. One day it came to the woman and asked, "Did God tell you not to eat fruit from any tree in the garden?"
[2] The woman answered, "God said we could eat fruit from any tree in the garden, [3] except the one in the middle. He told us not to eat fruit

from that tree or even to touch it. If we do, we will die."

⁴ "No, you won't!" the snake replied. ⁵ "God understands what will happen on the day you eat fruit from that tree. You will see what you have done, and you will know the difference between right and wrong, just as God does."

⁶ The woman stared at the fruit. It looked beautiful and tasty. She wanted the wisdom that it would give her, and she ate some of the fruit. Her husband was there with her, so she gave some to him, and he ate it too. ⁷ Right away they saw what they had done, and they realized they were naked. Then they sewed fig leaves together to make something to cover themselves.

⁸ Late in the afternoon a breeze began to blow, and the man and woman heard the LORD God walking in the garden. They were frightened and hid behind some trees.

⁹ The LORD called out to the man and asked, "Where are you?"

¹⁰ The man answered, "I was naked, and when I heard you walking through the garden, I was frightened and hid!"

¹¹ "How did you know you were naked?" God asked. "Did you eat any fruit from that tree in the middle of the garden?"

¹² "It was the woman you put here with me," the man said. "She gave me some of the fruit, and I ate it."

¹³ The LORD God then asked the woman, "What have you done?"

"The snake tricked me," she answered. "And I ate some of that fruit."

¹⁴ So the LORD God said to the snake:

> "Because of what you have done,
>> you will be the only animal
>> to suffer this curse—
> For as long as you live,
>> you will crawl on your stomach
> and eat dirt.
> ¹⁵ You and this woman
>> will hate each other;
>> your descendants and hers
>> will always be enemies.
>> One of hers will strike you
>> on the head,

and you will strike him
on the heel."

[16] Then the LORD said to the woman,

"You will suffer terribly
        when you give birth.
But you will still desire
        your husband,
        and he will rule over you."

[17] The LORD said to the man,

"You listened to your wife
        and ate fruit from that tree.
And so, the ground
        will be under a curse
        because of what you did.
As long as you live,
        you will have to struggle
        to grow enough food.
[18]   Your food will be plants,
        but the ground
        will produce
        thorns and thistles.
[19]   You will have to sweat
        to earn a living;
        you were made out of soil,
        and you will once again
        turn into soil."

[20] The man Adam named his wife Eve because she would become the
mother of all who live.
[21] Then the LORD God made clothes out of animal skins for the man
and his wife.
[22] The LORD said, "These people now know the difference between
right and wrong, just as we do. But they must not be allowed to eat
fruit from the tree that lets them live forever." [23] So the LORD God

sent them out of the Garden of Eden, where they would have to work the ground from which the man had been made. [24] Then God put winged creatures at the entrance to the garden and a flaming, flashing sword to guard the way to the life-giving tree.

Job 26:5-14
By God's Wisdom and Power
the Mighty Ocean was Conquered

True North: No matter how weary you are, no part of life or death is apart from God. That's what Job believed.

Job said:

[5]   Remember the terrible trembling
         of those in the world of the dead
                  below the mighty ocean.
[6]   Nothing in that land
         of death and destruction
                  is hidden from God,

7   who hung the northern sky
    and suspended the earth
            on empty space.
8   God stores water in clouds,
            but they don't burst,
9   and he wraps them around
            the face of the moon.
10 On the surface of the ocean,
    God has drawn a boundary line
            between light and darkness.
11 And columns supporting the sky
            tremble at his command.

12 By his power and wisdom,
    God conquered the force
            of the mighty ocean.
13 The heavens became bright
            when he breathed,
    and the escaping sea monster
            died at the hands of God.
14 These things are merely a whisper
            of God's power at work.
    How little we would understand
    if this whisper
            ever turned into thunder!

Job 38.1-38
Do People Command the Sea, or Does God?

True North: You have limits. So do we. These limits frustrate us and may even cause us to be fearful of living. It is good to know we have a God without limits who cares for us limits and all. That is what Job learned from God's answers to his complaints about his life.

38 From out of a storm,
            the Lord said to Job:
2   Why do you talk so much

3   when you know so little?
Now get ready to face me!
Can you answer
      the questions I ask?
4   How did I lay the foundation
for the earth?
      Were you there?
5   Doubtless you know who decided
      its length and width.
6   What supports the foundation?
Who placed the cornerstone,
7   while morning stars sang,
      and angels rejoiced?

8   When the ocean was born,
      I set its boundaries
9   and wrapped it in blankets
      of thickest fog.
10   Then I built a wall around it,
      locked the gates, 11 and said,
"Your powerful waves stop here!
      They can go no farther."

12   Did you ever tell the sun to rise?
      And did it obey?
13   Did it take hold of the earth
and shake out the wicked
      like dust from a rug?
14   Early dawn outlines the hills
like stitches on clothing
      or sketches on clay.
15   But its light is too much
for those who are evil,
      and their power is broken.

16   Job, have you ever walked
      on the ocean floor?
17   Have you seen the gate

to the world of the dead?
18 And how large is the earth?
Tell me, if you know!

19 Where is the home of light,
and where does darkness live?
20 Can you lead them home?
21 I'm certain you must be able to,
since you were already born
when I created everything.

22 Have you been to the places
where I keep snow and hail,
23 until I use them to punish
and conquer nations?
24 From where does lightning leap,
or the east wind blow?
25 Who carves out a path
for thunderstorms?
Who sends torrents of rain
26 on empty deserts
where no one lives?
27 Rain that changes barren land
to meadows green with grass.
28 Who is the father of the dew
and of the rain?
29 Who gives birth to the sleet
and the frost
30 that fall in winter,
when streams and lakes
freeze solid as a rock?

31 Can you arrange stars in groups
such as Orion
and the Pleiades?
32 Do you control the stars
or set in place the Big Dipper
and the Little Dipper?

33 Do you know the laws
        that govern the heavens,
   and can you make them rule
        the earth?
34 Can you order the clouds
        to send a downpour,
35 or will lightning flash
        at your command?
36 Did you teach birds to know
   that rain or floods
        are on their way?
37 Can you count the clouds
   or pour out their water
38   on the dry, lumpy soil?

Job 41.1-34
A Song God Sang About the Great Sea Monster

True North: As you sail, you've seen sea creatures like this that amaze and alarm you. They are not yours to control. Enjoy them, but do not harm them or pollute their waters. This sea monster would be more dangerous without God's control. See Psalm 74.12-17; Isaiah 26.21-27.9; Habbakuk 3.8-15.

41 Can you catch a sea monster
        by using a fishhook?
   Can you tie its mouth shut
        with a rope?
2 Can it be led around
   by a ring in its nose
        or a hook in its jaw?
3 Will it beg for mercy?
4 Will it surrender
        as a slave for life?
5 Can it be tied by the leg
   like a pet bird
        for little girls?

6   Is it ever chopped up
and its pieces bargained for
    in the fish-market?
7   Can it be killed
    with harpoons or spears?
8   Wrestle it just once —
    that will be the end.
9   Merely a glimpse of this monster
    makes all courage melt.
10 And if it is too fierce
for anyone to attack,
    who would dare oppose me?
11 I am in command of the world
    and in debt to no one.

12 What powerful legs,
what a stout body
    this monster possesses!
13 Who could strip off its armor
or bring it under control
    with a harness?
14 Who would try to open its jaws,
    full of fearsome teeth?

According to recent fossil studies, *Sacosuchus Imperator* or "flesh crocodile emperor," lived in the dinosaur era. Dubbed "SuperCroc," it was one of the largest crocodilians ever--weighing about ten tons. It even ate dinosaurs. Source: National Geographic Magazine.

15   Its back is covered
            with shield after shield,
16   firmly bound and closer together
17   than breath to breath.

18   When this monster sneezes,
     lightning flashes, and its eyes
            glow like the dawn.
19   Sparks and fiery flames
            explode from its mouth.
20   And smoke spews from its nose
     like steam
            from a boiling pot,
21   while its blazing breath
            scorches everything in sight.

22   Its neck is so tremendous
            that everyone trembles,
23   the weakest parts of its body
     are harder than iron,
24   and its heart is stone.
25   When this noisy monster appears,
     even the most powerful
            turn and run in fear.
26   No sword or spear can harm it,
27   and weapons of bronze or iron
            are as useless as straw
            or rotten wood.
28   Rocks thrown from a sling
     cause it no more harm
            than husks of grain.
     This monster fears no arrows,
29   it simply smiles at spears,
     and striking it with a stick
     is like slapping it with straw.

30   As it crawls through the mud,
     its sharp and spiny hide

tears the ground apart.
31 And when it swims down deep,
the sea starts churning
like boiling oil,
32 and it leaves behind a trail
of shining white foam.
33 No other creature on earth
is so fearless.
34 It is king of all proud creatures,
and it looks upon the others
as nothing.

Psalm 29.1-11
King David Praised God for Controlling the Waters

True North: Even a famous king like David knew he was not God's equal in power. Even if you are the captain of a ship you are still far from the power and authority God has. You can only be God's servant, not God's equal. Yet, that same powerful God wants to give you peace and calm waters!

1 All of you angels in heaven,
honor the glory and power
of the Lord
2 Honor the wonderful name
of the Lord
and worship the Lord
most holy and glorious.

3 The voice of the Lord
echoes over the oceans.
The glorious Lord God
thunders above the roar
of the raging sea,
4 and his voice is mighty
and marvelous.
5 The voice of the Lord
destroys the cedar trees;

the Lord shatters cedars
      on Mount Lebanon.
6   God makes Mount Lebanon
      skip like a calf
and Mount Hermon
      jump like a wild ox.

7   The voice of the Lord
makes lightning flash
8   and the desert tremble.
And because of the Lord
the desert near Kadesh
      shivers and shakes.

9   The voice of the Lord
makes deer give birth
      before their time.
Forests are stripped of leaves,
and the temple is filled
      with shouts of praise.

10   The Lord rules on his throne,
      king of the flood forever.
11   Pray that our Lord
will make us strong
      and give us peace.

Psalm 93.1-5
The Floods Praised God

True North: When you hear the oceans roar, they are praising God. When you hear the sea gulls' cry, they are praising God. Do not neglect to do what the creation around you does so joyfully.

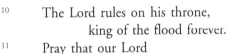

1   Our Lord you are King!
Majesty and power
      are your royal robes.

You put the world in place,
and it will never be moved.
2 You have always ruled,
and you are eternal.

3 The ocean is roaring, Lord
The sea is pounding hard.
4 Its mighty waves are majestic,
but you are more majestic,
and you rule over all.
5 Your decisions are firm,
and your temple will always
be beautiful and holy.

Psalm 98.1-9
Oceans, Roar! Rivers, Clap Your Hands!

True North: God will come to remove all oppression from the earth, including that which afflicts seafarers. Be ready to rejoice at God's steadfast love and righteousness!

1 Sing a new song to the Lord
He has worked miracles,
and with his own powerful arm,
he has won the victory.
2 The Lord has shown the nations
that he has the power to save
and to bring justice.
3 God has been faithful
in his love for Israel,
and his saving power is seen
everywhere on earth.

4 Tell everyone on this earth
to sing happy songs
in praise of the Lord.
5 Make music for him on harps.

Play beautiful melodies!
6 Sound the trumpets and horns
and celebrate with joyful songs
for our Lord and King!

7 Command the ocean to roar
with all of its creatures,
and the earth to shout
with all of its people.
8 Order the rivers
to clap their hands,
and all of the hills
to sing together.
9 Let them worship the Lord
He is coming to judge
everyone on the earth,
and he will be honest
and fair.

Psalm 104.1-30
God Formed Leviathan to Splash in the Sea!

True North: *Have you thought about God enjoying the creation? This psalm has. The great fish, Leviathan, as big as a whale, splashes its tail with great joy. Would God enjoy you less?*

1 I praise you, Lord God,
with all my heart.
You are glorious and majestic,
dressed in royal robes
2 and surrounded by light.
You spread out the sky
like a tent,
3 and you built your home
over the mighty ocean.
The clouds are your chariot
with the wind as its wings.

4   The winds are your messengers,
     and flames of fire
               are your servants.

5   You built foundations
     for the earth, and it
               will never be shaken.
6   You covered the earth
     with the ocean that rose
               above the mountains.
7   Then your voice thundered!
     And the water flowed
8   down the mountains
     and through the valleys
               to the place you prepared.
9   Now you have set boundaries,
     so that the water will never
               flood the earth again.

10   You provide streams of water
               in the hills and valleys,
11   so that the donkeys

and other wild animals
        can satisfy their thirst.

12 Birds build their nests nearby
        and sing in the trees.

13 From your home above
you send rain on the hills
        and water the earth.

14 You let the earth produce
        grass for cattle,
        plants for our food,

15   wine to cheer us up,
        olive oil for our skin,
        and grain for our health.

16 Our Lord your trees
        always have water,
and so do the cedars
        you planted in Lebanon.

17 Birds nest in those trees,
and storks make their home
        in the fir trees.

18 Wild goats find a home
        in the tall mountains,
and small animals can hide
        between the rocks.

19 You created the moon
        to tell us the seasons.
The sun knows when to set,

20   and you made the darkness,
so the animals in the forest
        could come out at night.

21 Lions roar as they hunt
        for the food you provide.

22 But when morning comes,
        they return to their dens,

23 then we go out to work
        until the end of day.

24 Our Lord by your wisdom
you made so many things;
the whole earth is covered
with your living creatures.

25 But what about the ocean
so big and wide?
It is alive with creatures,
large and small.

26 And there are the ships,
as well as Leviathan,
the monster you created
to splash in the sea.

27 All of these depend on you
to provide them with food,

28 and you feed each one
with your own hand,
until they are full.

29 But when you turn away,
they are terrified;
when you end their life,
they die and rot.

30 You created all of them
by your Spirit,
and you give new life
to the earth.

Psalm 148.1-14
All Waters Above the Sky, Praise God!

*True North: Feeling joyless? Make a list of everything that praises God.
Then thank each of them for their witness that you are blessed to share. Then
join them in praising and thanking God.*

1 Shout praises to the Lord
Shout the Lord's praises
in the highest heavens.

2   All of you angels,
    and all who serve him above,
            come and offer praise.

3   Sun and moon,
    and all of you bright stars,
            come and offer praise.
4   Highest heavens, and the water
    above the highest heavens,
            come and offer praise.

5   Let all things praise
            the name of the Lord
    because they were created
            at his command.
6   He made them to last forever,
    and nothing can change
            what he has done.

7   All creatures on earth,
    you obey his commands,
            so come praise the Lord!

8   Sea monsters and the deep sea,
    fire and hail, snow and frost,
            and every stormy wind,
            come praise the Lord!

9   All mountains and hills,
            fruit trees and cedars,
10 every wild and tame animal,
    all reptiles and birds,
            come praise the Lord!
11 Every king and every ruler,
            all nations on earth,
12 every man and every woman,
    young people and old,
            come praise the Lord!

13   All creation, come praise
the name of the Lord.
      Praise his name alone.
The glory of God is greater
      than heaven and earth.

14   Like a bull with mighty horns,
the Lord protects
      his faithful nation Israel,
because they belong to him.
      Shout praises to the Lord!

Amos 5.8-9
God Formed the Stars to Sail By

*True North: God formed the stars by whose light and direction the first
seafarers found their way to safe harbor. Whenever you are at sea at night, look
up and know God was thinking about seafarers' and fishers' needs so long ago.*

8   But the Lord created the stars
      and put them in place.
He turns darkness to dawn
      and daylight to darkness;
he scoops up the ocean
      and empties it on the earth.
9   God destroys mighty soldiers
      and strong fortresses.

How God Directed the Waters
to Save People and Make Believers

Noah and Moses Saved
from the Sea

Genesis 6.5-8.22
Noah's Seafaring Story
God Punished the Earth by Flood Because of Evil People
God Helped Noah Become a Shipbuilder
and Seafarer to Save His Family.

True North: This is a most exciting reading about God's faithfulness and concern about the evils that bring people to despair. It also lets you know that God thinks about what the Almighty has done and considers the consequences for the earth. Since God thinks deeply and honestly about God's past actions, you have the freedom to do so too. So, feel free to share your griefs and hopes with your Lord.

Wickedness Brings God to Action

⁵ The Lord saw how bad the people on earth were and that everything they thought and planned was evil. ⁶ He was very sorry that he had made them, ⁷ and he said, "I'll destroy every living creature on earth! I'll wipe out people, animals, birds, and reptiles. I'm sorry I ever made them."

⁸ But the Lord was pleased with Noah, ⁹ and this is the story about him. Noah was the only person who lived right and obeyed God. ¹⁰ He had three sons: Shem, Ham, and Japheth.

¹¹⁻¹² God knew that everyone was terribly cruel and violent. ¹³ So he told Noah:

Cruelty and violence have spread everywhere. Now I'm going to destroy the whole earth and all its people. ¹⁴ Get some good lumber and build a boat. Put rooms in it and cover it with tar inside and out. ¹⁵ Make it four hundred fifty feet long, seventy-five feet wide, and forty-five feet high. ¹⁶ Build a roof on the boat and leave a space of about eighteen inches between the roof and the sides. Make the boat three stories high and put a door on one side.

¹⁷ I'm going to send a flood that will destroy everything that breathes! Nothing will be left alive. ¹⁸ But I solemnly promise that you, your wife, your sons, and your daughters-in-law will be kept safe in the boat.

¹⁹⁻²⁰ Bring into the boat with you a male and a female of every kind of animal and bird, as well as a male and a female of every reptile.

I don't want them to be destroyed. [21] Store up enough food both for yourself and for them.

[22] Noah did everything the Lord told him to do.

7 *The Flood*

The Lord told Noah:

Take your whole family with you into the boat, because you are the only one on this earth who pleases me. [2] Take seven pairs of every kind of animal that can be used for sacrifice and one pair of all others. [3] Also take seven pairs of every kind of bird with you. Do this so there will always be animals and birds on the earth. [4] Seven days from now I will send rain that will last for forty days and nights, and I will destroy all other living creatures I have made.

[5-7] Noah was six hundred years old when he went into the boat to escape the flood, and he did everything the Lord had told him to do. His wife, his sons, and his daughters-in-law all went inside with him. [8-9] He obeyed God and took a male and a female of each kind of animal and bird into the boat with him. [10] Seven days later a flood began to cover the earth.

[11-12] Noah was six hundred years old when the water under the earth started gushing out everywhere. The sky opened like windows, and rain poured down for forty days and nights. All this began on the seventeenth day of the second month of the year. [13] On that day Noah and his wife went into the boat with their three sons, Shem, Ham, and Japheth, and their wives. [14] They took along every kind of animal, tame and wild, including the birds. [15] Noah took a male and a female of every living creature with him, [16] just as God had told him to do. And when they were all in the boat, God closed the door.

[17-18] For forty days the rain poured down without stopping. And the water became deeper and deeper, until the boat started floating high above the ground. [19-20] Finally, the mighty flood was so deep that even the highest mountain peaks were almost twenty-five feet below the surface of the water. [21] Not a bird, animal, reptile, or human was left alive anywhere on earth. [22-23] The Lord destroyed everything that breathed. Nothing was left alive except Noah and the others in the boat. [24] A hundred fifty days later, the water started going down.

God remembered those sailing the ark
and blessed them with safe harbor and a promise.

8 God did not forget about Noah and the animals with him in the boat. So God made a wind blow, and the water started going down. ² God stopped up the places where the water had been gushing out from under the earth. He also closed up the sky, and the rain stopped. ³ For one hundred fifty days the water slowly went down. ⁴ Then on the seventeenth day of the seventh month of the year, the boat came to rest somewhere in the Ararat mountains. ⁵ The water kept going down, and the mountain tops could be seen on the first day of the tenth month.

⁶⁻⁷ Forty days later Noah opened a window to send out a raven, but it kept flying around until the water had dried up. ⁸ Noah wanted to find out if the water had gone down, and he sent out a dove. ⁹ Deep water was still everywhere, and the dove could not find a place to land. So it flew back to the boat. Noah held out his hand and helped it back in.

¹⁰ Seven days later Noah sent the dove out again. ¹¹ It returned in the evening, holding in its beak a green leaf from an olive tree. Noah knew that the water was finally going down. ¹² He waited seven more days before sending the dove out again, and this time it did not return.

¹³ Noah was now six hundred one years old. And by the first day of that year, almost all the water had gone away. Noah made an

opening in the roof of the boat and saw that the ground was getting dry. [14] By the twenty-seventh day of the second month, the earth was completely dry.

[15] God said to Noah, [16] "You, your wife, your sons, and your daughters-in-law may now leave the boat. [17] Let out the birds, animals, and reptiles, so they can mate and live all over the earth." [18] After Noah and his family had gone out of the boat, [19] the living creatures left in groups of their own kind.

[20] Noah built an altar where he could offer sacrifices to the Lord. Then he offered on the altar one of each kind of animal and bird that could be used for a sacrifice. [21] The smell of the burning offering pleased God, and he said:

Never again will I punish the earth for the sinful things its people do. All of them have evil thoughts from the time they are young, but I will never destroy everything that breathes, as I did this time.

[22] As long as the earth remains,
there will be planting
> and harvest,
> cold and heat;
> winter and summer,
> day and night.

Exodus 14.1-31
God Rescued the Israelites by Parting the Red Sea

True North: This is a great story of God's action to rescue people from oppression. The mighty king cannot withstand God's call to the waters to divide and rise against the king. Take courage from the lengths God will go to save people from slavery and racism. God will lead you out of bondage! Read also these reflections on the escape from Egypt: Psalm 63.7-14, 66.5-7, 77.1-20, 124.1-8.

14 At Etham the Lord said to Moses:

[2] Tell the people of Israel to turn back and camp across from Pi-Hahiroth near Baal-Zephon, between Migdol and the Red Sea. [3] The king will think they were afraid to cross the desert and that they are

wandering around, trying to find another way to leave the country. ⁴ I will make the king stubborn again, and he will try to catch you. Then I will destroy him and his army. People everywhere will praise me for my victory, and the Egyptians will know that I really am the Lord.

The Israelites obeyed the Lord and camped where he told them.

⁵ When the king of Egypt heard that the Israelites had finally left, he and his officials changed their minds and said, "Look what we have done! We let them get away, and they will no longer be our slaves."

⁶ The king got his war chariot and army ready. ⁷ He commanded his officers in charge of his six hundred best chariots and all his other chariots to start after the Israelites. ⁸ The Lord made the king so stubborn that he went after them, even though the Israelites proudly went on their way. ⁹ But the king's horses and chariots and soldiers caught up with them while they were camping by the Red Sea near Pi-Hahiroth and Baal-Zephon.

¹⁰ When the Israelites saw the king coming with his army, they were frightened and begged the Lord for help. ¹¹ They also complained to Moses, "Wasn't there enough room in Egypt to bury us? Is that why you brought us out here to die in the desert? Why did you bring us out of Egypt anyway? ¹² While we were there, didn't we tell you to leave us alone? We had rather be slaves in Egypt than die in this desert!"

¹³ But Moses answered, "Don't be afraid! Be brave, and you will see the Lord save you today. These Egyptians will never bother you again. ¹⁴ The Lord will fight for you, and you won't have to do a thing."

¹⁵ The Lord said to Moses, "Why do you keep calling out to me for help? Tell the Israelites to move forward. ¹⁶ Then hold your walking stick over the sea. The water will open up and make a road where they can walk through on dry ground. ¹⁷ I will make the Egyptians so stubborn that they will go after you. Then I will be praised because of what happens to the king and his chariots and cavalry. ¹⁸ The Egyptians will know for sure that I am the Lord."

¹⁹ All this time God's angel had gone ahead of Israel's army, but now he moved behind them. A large cloud had also gone ahead of them, ²⁰ but now it moved between the Egyptians and the Israelites.

The cloud gave light to the Israelites, but made it dark for the Egyptians, and during the night they could not come any closer.

[21] Moses stretched his arm over the sea, and the Lord sent a strong east wind that blew all night until there was dry land where the water had been. The sea opened up, [22] and the Israelites walked through on dry land with a wall of water on each side.

[23] The Egyptian chariots and cavalry went after them. [24] But before daylight the Lord looked down at the Egyptian army from the fiery cloud and made them panic. [25] Their chariot wheels got stuck, and it was hard for them to move. So the Egyptians said to one another, "Let's leave these people alone! The Lord is on their side and is fighting against us."

[26] The Lord told Moses, "Stretch your arm toward the sea — the water will cover the Egyptians and their cavalry and chariots." [27] Moses stretched out his arm, and at daybreak the water rushed toward the Egyptians. They tried to run away, but the Lord drowned them in the sea. [28] The water came and covered the chariots, the cavalry, and the whole Egyptian army that had followed the Israelites into the sea. Not one of them was left alive. [29] But the sea had made a wall of water on each side of the Israelites; so they walked through on dry land.

[30] On that day, when the Israelites saw the bodies of the Egyptians washed up on the shore, they knew that the Lord had saved them. [31] Because of the mighty power he had used against the Egyptians, the Israelites worshiped him and trusted him and his servant Moses.

Exodus 15:1-21
The Victory Songs of Moses and Miriam

True North: When Mexican and Spanish sailors were in danger of shipwreck, they made vows to God that they would have a painting made after their rescue to show how God answered their prayers and saved them from death. These ex-voto paintings were displayed in churches to witness to the power of God to save. Ex-voto means something done because of a vow. Once you are rescued from disaster, it is good to praise the one who rescued you, telling and showing everyone what God has done. Remember to thank God for the other sailors who acted quickly to help. Remember also to ask God to comfort the families, friends and colleagues of any who were lost at sea.

15 Moses and the Israelites sang this song in praise of the Lord:
> I sing praises to the Lord
>> for his great victory!
>
> He has thrown the horses
> and their riders
>> into the sea.

2
> The Lord is my strength,
> the reason for my song,
>> because he has saved me.
>
> I praise and honor the Lord —
> he is my God and the God
>> of my ancestors.

3
> The Lord is his name,
>> and he is a warrior!

4
> He threw the chariots and army
> of Egypt's king
>> into the Red Sea,
>
> and he drowned the best
>> of the king's officers.

5
> They sank to the bottom
>> just like stones.

6
> With the tremendous force
> of your right arm, our Lord,

        you crushed your enemies.

7   What a great victory was yours,
as you defeated everyone
        who opposed you.
Your fiery anger wiped them out,
        as though they were straw.

8   You were so furious
that the sea piled up
        like a wall,
and the ocean depths
        curdled like cheese.

9   Your enemies boasted
        that they would
pursue and capture us,
divide up our possessions,
treat us as they wished,
then take out their swords
        and kill us right there.

10   But when you got furious,
they sank like lead,
        swallowed by ocean waves.

11   Our Lord, no other gods
compare with you —
        Majestic and holy!
        Fearsome and glorious!
        Miracle worker!

12   When you signaled
        with your right hand,
your enemies were swallowed
        deep into the earth.

13   The people you rescued
were led by your powerful love
        to your holy place.

14   Nations learned of this
        and trembled —
Philistines shook with horror.

15   The leaders of Edom and of Moab
        were terrified.
    Everyone in Canaan fainted,
16   struck down by fear.
    Our Lord, your powerful arm
        kept them still as a rock
    until the people you rescued
    for your very own
        had marched by.

17   You will let your people settle
        on your chosen mountain,
    where you built your home
        and your temple.
18   Our Lord, you will rule forever!

19 The Lord covered the royal Egyptian cavalry and chariots with the sea, after the Israelites had walked safely through on dry ground. 20 Miriam the sister of Aaron was a prophet. So she took her tambourine and led the other women out to play their tambourines and to dance. 21 Then she sang to them:

    "Sing praises to the Lord
        for his great victory!
    He has thrown the horses
    and their riders into the sea."

How God Directed the Waters
to Save People and Make Believers

Sea Readings from Torah and Psalms

Torah is the name given to the first five books of the Old Testament: Genesis, Exodus, Leviticus, Numbers and Deuteronomy.

Numbers 34.1-12
Just as Great Rivers Limited Eden, So the Seas Limit Israel

True North: Moses, who parted the Red Sea by God's power, also defined the boundaries of Israel by the seas. All human life is limited by the awesome power of the sea. The book of Revelation tells us that at the end of time, the sea will give up our long-lost beloved seafarers, and become like glass: its beauty preserved but its danger gone. It is good to know that God has protected us until then with the gift of dry land. Read Revelation 4.6; 15.2.

34 The Lord told Moses [2] to tell the people of Israel that their land in Canaan would have the following borders:

[3] The southern border will be the Zin Desert and the northwest part of Edom. This border will begin at the south end of the Dead Sea. [4] It will go west from there, but will turn southward to include Scorpion Pass, the village of Zin, and the town of Kadesh-Barnea. From there, the border will continue to Hazar-Addar and on to Azmon. [5] It will run along the Egyptian Gorge and end at the Mediterranean Sea.

[6] The western border will be the Mediterranean Sea.

[7] The northern border will begin at the Mediterranean, then continue eastward to Mount Hor. [8] After that, it will run to Lebo-Hamath and across to Zedad, which is the northern edge of your land. [9] From Zedad, the border will continue east to Ziphron and end at Hazar-Enan.

[10] The eastern border will begin at Hazar-Enan in the north, then run south to Shepham, [11] and on down to Riblah on the east side of Ain. From there, it will go south to the eastern hills of Lake Galilee,

[12] then follow the Jordan River down to the north end of the Dead Sea.

The land within those four borders will belong to you.

2 Samuel 14.14
Although People are as Weak as Water
God Will Restore Us

True North: From Genesis on, our lives are marked by death. For example, our first parents, Adam and Eve, were too weak to bear the shame of their own arrogance toward God. God protected them with clothes and gave them children to balance out death's attacks (Gn 2:1-3:24). God loves and protects you in your weakness. So, there is no need to hide from God and pretend that God doesn't know all about you already! God loves you still!

[14] We each must die and disappear like water poured out on the ground. But God doesn't take our lives. Instead, he figures out ways of bringing us back when we run away.

2 Samuel 22.1-19
David Praised God for Rescuing Him
From the Waves of Death

True North: David the king, prophet and psalmist thought of this terrible attack by his enemies to be as frightening as drowning. And yet the Lord saved him and he lived to praise God. Sea also Psalm 69.1-36.

22 David sang a song to the Lord after the Lord had rescued him from his enemies, especially Saul. These are the words to David's song:
[2]   Our Lord and our God,
        you are my mighty rock,
            my fortress, my protector.
[3]   You are the rock
            where I am safe.
        You are my shield,

my powerful weapon,
and my place of shelter.

You rescue me and keep me
from being hurt.
4 I praise you, our Lord!
I prayed to you,
and you rescued me
from my enemies.
5 Death, like ocean waves,
surrounded me,
and I was almost swallowed
by its flooding waters.

6 Ropes from the world
of the dead
had coiled around me,
and death had set a trap
in my path.
7 I was in terrible trouble
when I called out to you,
but from your temple
you heard me
and answered my prayer.
8 Earth shook and shivered!
The columns supporting the sky
rocked back and forth.
You were angry
9 and breathed out smoke.
Scorching heat and fiery flames
spewed from your mouth.

10 You opened the heavens
like curtains,
and you came down
with storm clouds
under your feet.
11 You rode on the backs

of flying creatures.
You appeared
with the wind as wings.
12 Darkness was your tent!
Thunderclouds filled the sky,
hiding you from sight.
13 Fiery coals lit up the sky
in front of you.

14 Lord Most High, your voice
thundered from the heavens.
15 You scattered your enemies
with arrows of lightning.
16 You roared at the sea,
and its deepest channels
could be seen.
You snorted,
and the earth shook
to its foundations.

17 You reached down from heaven,
and you lifted me

from deep in the ocean.
18   You rescued me from enemies
who were hateful
and too powerful for me.
19   On the day disaster struck,
they came and attacked,
but you defended me.

Psalm 23.1-6
God Leads us to Peaceful Waters Despite Death-Dark Valleys

True North: This well-beloved psalm of King David shows how he felt guided by God toward refreshment in everything he did. Even in the midst of his enemies, God set a feast for him. When your Chaplains bring you the bread and the wine of the Lord's Supper on board your ship, they are bringing you the feast of God.

1   You, Lord are my shepherd.
     I will never be in need.
2   You let me rest in fields
    of green grass.
You lead me to streams
of peaceful water,
3   and you refresh my life.

You are true to your name,
and you lead me
    along the right paths.
4   I may walk through valleys
as dark as death,
    but I won't be afraid.
You are with me,
and your shepherd's rod
    makes me feel safe.

5   You treat me to a feast,
    while my enemies watch.

You honor me as your guest,
and you fill my cup
      until it overflows.
6   Your kindness and love
will always be with me
      each day of my life,
and I will live forever
in your house, Lord.

Psalm 46.1-11
God is Our Refuge Amid Seaquakes and Provides Glad Waters

True North: *The 16th century church reformer, Martin Luther, rewrote this psalm into a much loved song about Christ. You may want to compare Luther's hymn to the Psalm. Luther has made the raging flood of the Psalm into the rage of sin or Satan.*

A mighty fortress is our God, A bulwark never failing;
Our helper He, amid the flood of mortal ills prevailing:
For still our ancient foe doth seek to work us woe; His craft and power are great,
And, armed with cruel hate, On earth is not his equal.

Did we in our own strength confide, our striving would be losing,
Were not the right Man on our side, the man of God's own choosing:
Dost ask who that may be? Christ Jesus, it is He; Lord Sabaoth His name,
From age to age the same, and He must win the battle.

And though this world, with devils filled, should threaten to undo us,
We will not fear, for God hath willed His truth to triumph through us:
The Prince of Darkness grim, we tremble not for him; his rage we can endure,
For lo, his doom is sure; one little word shall fell him.

That word above all earthly powers, No thanks to them, abideth;
The Spirit and the gifts are ours through him who with us sideth:
Let goods and kindred go, this mortal life also; the body they may kill:
God's truth abideth still; His kingdom is forever.

[A special song for the people of Korah and for the music leader.]

¹God is our mighty fortress,
        always ready to help
                in times of trouble.
2   And so, we won't be afraid!
                Let the earth tremble
        and the mountains tumble
                into the deepest sea.
3   Let the ocean roar and foam,
        and its raging waves
                shake the mountains.

4   A river and its streams
                bring joy to the city,
        which is the sacred home
                of God Most High.
5   God is in that city,
        and it won't be shaken.
                He will help it at dawn.

6   Nations rage! Kingdoms fall!
        But at the voice of God
                the earth itself melts.
7   The Lord All-Powerful
                is with us.
        The God of Jacob
                is our fortress.

8   Come! See the fearsome things
                the Lord has done on earth.
9   God brings wars to an end
                all over the world.
        He breaks the arrows,
        shatters the spears,
                and burns the shields.
10   Our God says, "Calm down,
                and learn that I am God!

All nations on earth
  will honor me."

11 The Lord All-Powerful
   is with us.
  The God of Jacob
   is our fortress.

Psalm 65.1-13
God Gives Hope to People Across the Sea

*True North: God answers prayer! Even the prayers of those across the sea!
That is good news. And when our sins overwhelm us, God forgives us! Read also
Psalm 8:6-8.*

1 Our God, you deserve praise
  in Zion, where we keep
   our promises to you.
2 Everyone will come to you
   because you answer prayer.
3 Our terrible sins get us down,
   but you forgive us.
4 You bless your chosen ones,
   and you invite them
  to live near you
   in your temple.
  We will enjoy your house,
   the sacred temple.
5 Our God, you save us,
  and your fearsome deeds answer
   our prayers for justice!
  You give hope to people
  everywhere on earth,
   even those across the sea.
6 You are strong,
  and your mighty power
   put the mountains in place.

7   You silence the roaring waves
and the noisy shouts
     of the nations.
8   People far away marvel
     at your fearsome deeds,
and all who live under the sun
celebrate and sing
     because of you.

9   You take care of the earth
and send rain to help the soil
     grow all kinds of crops.
Your rivers never run dry,
and you prepare the earth
     to produce much grain.
10   You water all of its fields
     and level the lumpy ground.
You send showers of rain
to soften the soil
     and help the plants sprout.
11   Wherever your footsteps
touch the earth,
     a rich harvest is gathered.
12   Desert pastures blossom,
     and mountains celebrate.
13   Meadows are filled
     with sheep and goats;

valleys overflow with grain
    and echo with joyful songs.

Psalm 107.23-43
Some of You Made a Living on the Sea
and Saw God's Wonders

True North: The sea can be overwhelming. Its beauty and might can look like chaos and frighten even the bravest seafarer. This sailor's psalm assures you that God will bless those who make their living from the sea, raise them up when they are needy and help their families to prosper.

23   Some of you made a living
        by sailing the mighty sea,
24   and you saw the miracles
        the Lord performed there.
25   At his command a storm arose,
        and waves covered the sea.
26   You were tossed to the sky
        and to the ocean depths,
    until things looked so bad
        that you lost your courage.
27   You staggered like drunkards
        and gave up all hope.
28   You were in serious trouble,
    but you prayed to the Lord
        and he rescued you.
29   He made the storm stop
        and the sea be quiet.
30   You were happy because of this,
    and he brought you to the port
        where you wanted to go.

31   You should praise the Lord
        for his love
    and for the wonderful things
        he does for all of us.

32   Honor the Lord
when you and your leaders
   meet to worship.

33   If you start doing wrong,
the Lord will turn rivers
   into deserts,
34   flowing streams
   into scorched land,
and fruitful fields
   into beds of salt.

35   But the Lord can also turn
   deserts into lakes
and scorched land
   into flowing streams.
36   If you are hungry,
you can settle there
   and build a town.
37   You can plant fields
and vineyards that produce
   a good harvest.
38   The Lord will bless you
with many children
   and with herds of cattle.

39   Sometimes you may be crushed
   by troubles and sorrows,
until only a few of you
   are left to survive.
40   But the Lord will take revenge
   on those who conquer you,
and he will make them wander
   across desert sands.
41   When you are suffering
   and in need,
he will come to your rescue,
and your families will grow

42 as fast as a herd of sheep.
You will see this because
    you obey the Lord
but everyone who is wicked
    will be silenced.

43 Be wise! Remember this
and think about the kindness
    of the Lord.

Psalm 114.1-8
Just as God Parted the Chaotic Waters to
Make a Home for All Creation, so God Parted the
Red Sea to Make a Home for Israel and Judah

True North: Mercy and grace do not come just once. God repeats good gifts again and again!

1 God brought his people
out of Egypt, that land
    with a strange language.
2 He made Judah his holy place
    and ruled over Israel.

3 When the sea looked at God,
        it ran away,
and the Jordan River
        flowed upstream.
4 The mountains and the hills
        skipped around like goats.

5 Ask the sea why it ran away
or ask the Jordan
        why it flowed upstream.
6 Ask the mountains and the hills
        why they skipped like goats!

7 Earth, you will tremble,
   when the Lord God of
         Jacob comes near,
8 because he turns solid rock
   into flowing streams
         and pools of water.

SEA READINGS FROM THE OLD TESTAMENT

How God Directed the Waters to Save People and Make Believers

Sea Readings from the Prophets

The prophets spoke to the kingdoms of Israel and Judah in times of grave national danger. The people of these kingdoms believed in God, but bad leadership, false prophets and marching armies regularly harmed them. The writings of the prophets are very direct in their judgments about evil neighboring empires like Assyria and ancient Egypt. The prophets understood that God might guide marching armies from some kingdoms to conquer the arrogance of others for the sake of all nations. God knew that all nations, even Israel, could fall short of the glory of God.

Isaiah 19.1-8
God Will Dry Up the Rivers of Egypt in Punishment for its Evil

True North: This is an oracle about the empire of Egypt. Must God work as hard to get your attention as was necessary to get Egypt's attention? Sometimes the worse things are, the closer God is to getting through to a stubborn you. Think about it!

19   This is a message
     about Egypt:
   The Lord comes to Egypt,
     riding swiftly on a cloud.
   The people are weak from fear.
   Their idols tremble
     as he approaches and says,
2   "I will punish Egypt
     with civil war —
   neighbors, cities, and kingdoms
     will fight each other.

3   "Egypt will be discouraged
     when I confuse their plans.
   They will try to get advice
     from their idols,
   from the spirits of the dead,
     and from fortunetellers.
4   I will put the Egyptians
   under the power of a cruel,
     heartless king.
   I, the Lord All-Powerful,
     have promised this."

5   The Nile River will dry up
     and become parched land.
6   Its streams will stink,
     Egypt will have no water,
   and the reeds and tall grass

7   will dry up.
Fields along the Nile
will be completely barren;
       every plant will disappear.

8   Those who fish in the Nile
will be discouraged
       and mourn.

Isaiah 33.17-24
You Who are Evil Destroyers are Like a Poorly Rigged Ship

True North: Isaiah was surely a sailor to have written this prophecy about rigging! Isaiah prophesied that the sea peoples would ultimately fail to conquer God's holy city, Jerusalem, and its people. In this reading, the prophet addressed three groups: 1) the people of Jerusalem (33.17-21), 2) the defeated enemy (33.23), 3) the injured and poor from the siege of Jerusalem (33.23b-24). If Isaiah thought of a confident believer as a well-rigged ship, then we'd have to think about a confident believer as a diesel engine in a super tanker. Does that sound like you? What part of you needs a hope overhaul? A talk aboard ship with a chaplain or ministering seafarer or a visit to a Bethel Center can be your dry dock for a faith tune-up.

Isaiah addresses the people of Jerusalem:

17   With your own eyes
you will see the glorious King;
       you will see his kingdom
       reaching far and wide.
18   Then you will ask yourself,
       "Where are those officials
who terrified us and forced us
       to pay such heavy taxes?"
19   You will never again have to see
       the proud people who spoke
a strange and foreign language

you could not understand.

20   Look to Mount Zion
where we celebrate
            our religious festivals.
You will see Jerusalem,
            secure as a tent with pegs
that cannot be pulled up
and fastened with ropes
            that can never be broken.

21   Our wonderful Lord
            will be with us!
There will be deep rivers
and wide streams
            safe from enemy ships.

22   The Lord is our judge
            and our ruler;
the Lord is our king
            and will keep us safe.

Isaiah addresses the enemy:
23   But your nation is a ship
            with its rigging loose,
its mast shaky,
            and its sail not spread.

Isaiah addresses the injured of Jerusalem:
> Someday even you that are lame
> will take everything you want
>> from your enemies.

24   The Lord will forgive your sins,
> and none of you will say,
>> "I feel sick."

Isaiah 42.1-12
Tell Those Who Sail the Ocean to Join in the Praise!

True North: Our Creator wanted justice for all people and chose one servant to bring that about. Isaiah was especially charged to tell seafarers that this good news was for them. What is it about seafaring that God would especially want you to hear the good news of this passage? Christians have always believed that when Isaiah was speaking about God's servant in his own time, he was also speaking about God's servant, Jesus Christ. More good news for seafarers! Read Acts 13:13-41 for the seafaring Chaplain Paul's witness to Jesus as God's suffering servant.

42   Here is my servant!
> I have made him strong.
> He is my chosen one;
> I am pleased with him.
> I have given him my Spirit,
>> and he will bring justice
>> to the nations.

2   He won't shout or yell
>> or call out in the streets.

3   He won't break off a bent reed
>> or put out a dying flame,
>> but he will make sure
>> that justice is done.

4   He won't quit or give up
>> until he brings justice
>> everywhere on earth,

and people in foreign nations
long for his teaching.

5   I am the LORD God.
     I created the heavens
                 like an open tent above.
     I made the earth and everything
                 that grows on it.
     I am the source of life
                 for all who live on this earth,
                 so listen to what I say.
6   I chose you to bring justice,
                 and I am here at your side.
     I selected and sent you
                 to bring light
                 and my promise of hope
                 to the nations.
7   You will give sight
                 to the blind;
                 you will set prisoners free
                 from dark dungeons.

8   My name is the LORD!
     I won't let idols or humans
                 share my glory and praise.
9   Everything has happened
                 just as I said it would;
                 now I will announce
                 what will happen next.
     Sing Praises to the LORD
10   Tell the whole world to sing
                 a new song to the LORD!
     Tell those who sail the ocean
                 and those who live far away
                 to join in the praise.
11   Tell the tribes of the desert
                 and everyone in the mountains
                 to celebrate and sing.

¹² Let them announce
　　　　　his praises everywhere.

Isaiah 44.1-8
God Will Pour Water and
the Holy Spirit on Thirsty Believers

True North: *This image of the stream of water on the land and pouring of the Holy Spirit on Jacob's and Israel's descendents is fulfilled in Christian baptism. Water and the Spirit come together with the Word of God. This first happened at the baptism of Jesus Christ.*

44 People of Israel,
　　　　I have chosen you
　　　　　　　as my servant.
² I am your Creator.
　　　　You were in my care
　　　　　　　even before you were born.
　　　　Israel, don't be terrified!
　　　　You are my chosen servant,
　　　　　　　my very favorite.

³ I will bless the thirsty land
　　　　　　　by sending streams of water;
　　　　I will bless your descendants
　　　　　　　by giving them my Spirit.
⁴ They will spring up like grass
　　　　or like willow trees
　　　　　　　near flowing streams.
⁵ They will worship me
　　　　　　　and become my people.
　　　　They will write my name
　　　　　　　on the back of their hands.
⁶ I am the Lord All-Powerful,
　　　　the first and the last,
　　　　　　　the one and only God.

Israel, I have rescued you!
   I am your King.
7 Can anyone compare with me?
If so, let them speak up
   and tell me now.
Let them say what has happened
since I made my nation
   long ago,
and let them tell
   what is going to happen.
8 Don't tremble with fear!
Didn't I tell you long ago?
   Didn't you hear me?
I alone am God —
no one else is a mighty rock.

Isaiah 48.16b-22
If You had Obeyed,
You Would have had Rivers of Prosperity

True North: It isn't only enemies who disobey the Lord God. So do believers. It is so much better to listen to the Lord. Let God's wisdom guide you toward safety and happiness.

By the power of his Spirit
the Lord God has sent me
17   with this message:
People of Israel,
I am the holy Lord God,
   the one who rescues you.
For your own good,
I teach you, and I lead you
   along the right path.
18 How I wish that you
   had obeyed my commands!
Your success and good fortune

would then have overflowed
like a flooding river.
19 Your nation would be blessed
with more people
than there are grains of sand
along the seashore.
And I would never have let
your country be destroyed.

20 Now leave Babylon!
Celebrate as you go.
Be happy and shout
for everyone to hear,
"The Lord has rescued
his servant Israel!
21 He led us through the desert
and made water flow from a rock
to satisfy our thirst.
22 But the Lord has promised
that none who are evil
will live in peace."

Isaiah 51.1-11
People Across the Sea
Eagerly Wait for Me to Rescue Them

True North: God promised Abraham and Sarah as many heirs as the stars in the heavens and as the grains of sand along the beach. Through this gift to Sarah and Abraham, God chose to include the people of the whole world under divine rule. God decided long ago to correct, guide, judge and love all nations and their peoples. Read more about God's concern for all the nations at Genesis 22.15-17; Amos 9.5-8.

Isaiah advises the people:
51 If you want to do right
and obey the Lord,

follow Abraham's example.
He was the rock from which
you were chipped.

2 God chose Abraham and Sarah
to be your ancestors.
The Lord blessed Abraham,
and from that one man
came many descendants.

3 Though Zion is in ruins,
the Lord will bring comfort,
and the city will be as lovely
as the garden of Eden
that he provided.
Then Zion will celebrate;
it will be thankful
and sing joyful songs.

The Lord wants the people to listen and watch:
4 The Lord says:
You are my people and nation!
So pay attention to me.
My teaching will cause justice
to shine like a light
for every nation.

5 Those who live across the sea
are eagerly waiting
for me to rescue them.
I am strong and ready;
soon I will come to save
and to rule all nations.

6 Look closely at the sky!
Stare at the earth.
The sky will vanish like smoke;
the earth will wear out
like clothes.
Everyone on this earth

will die like flies.
But my victory will last;
my saving power never ends.

7   If you want to do right
         and to obey my teaching
with all your heart,
         then pay close attention.
Don't be discouraged
when others insult you
         and say hurtful things.
8   They will be eaten away
         like a moth-eaten coat.
But my victory will last;
my saving power
         will never end.

Isaiah asks the Lord to act quickly:
    Wake up! Do something, Lord.
         Be strong and ready.
    Wake up! Do what you did
         for our people long ago.
    Didn't you chop up
         Rahab the monster?
10   Didn't you dry up the deep sea
and make a road for your people
         to follow safely across?
11   Now those you have rescued
will return to Jerusalem,

singing on their way.
They will be crowned
with great happiness,
never again to be burdened
with sadness and sorrow.

Isaiah 54.1-10
As I Swore to Noah After the Flood,
I Will Not Reject You

True North: God swore a promise to Noah never to destroy the world by water again. Here God promises not to be angry again with Judah and Israel. That same promise holds for all others who feel that God is angry with them: the childless woman, the orphan, and the seafarer. For God is your spouse, your parent, your compass and your redeemer. God has promised to stay in a loving relationship with you. Do you promise too?

54 Sing and shout,
even though you have never
had children!
The Lord has promised that you
will have more children
than someone married
for a long time.
2   Make your tents larger!
Spread out the tent pegs;
fasten them firmly.
3   You and your descendants
will take over the land
of other nations.
You will settle in towns
that are now in ruins.

4   Don't be afraid or ashamed
and don't be discouraged.
You won't be disappointed.

Forget how sinful you were
     when you were young;
stop feeling ashamed
     for being left a widow.
5 The Lord All-Powerful,
the Holy God of Israel,
     rules all the earth.
He is your Creator and husband,
     and he will rescue you.
6 You were like a young wife,
     brokenhearted and crying
because her husband
     had divorced her.
But the Lord your God says,
     "I am taking you back!
7 I rejected you for a while,
     but with love and tenderness
I will embrace you again.
8 For a while, I turned away
     in furious anger.
Now I will have mercy
     and love you forever!
I, your protector and Lord,
     make this promise."
9 I once promised Noah that I
     would never again destroy
     the earth by a flood.
Now I have promised that I
     will never again
     get angry
     and punish you.
10 Every mountain and hill
     may disappear.
But I will always be kind
     and merciful to you;
I won't break my agreement
     to give your nation peace.

Jeremiah 2.9-13
You Have Forsaken God's Fountain for a Cracked Cistern

True North: So, why dig a pit where no water flows when God's fresh spring is so near? Usually because we are afraid or stubborn. What things happen to you that make you think of turning away from God? What useless wells have you dug? How did God get you to turn back to living water? For another example of human stubbornness using water words, read Jeremiah 5.20-25.

God speaks,

9   I will take you to court
      and accuse you
           and your descendants
10   of a crime that no nation
          has ever committed before.
      Just ask anyone, anywhere,
      from the eastern deserts
          to the islands in the west.
11   You will find that no nation
      has ever abandoned its gods
          even though they were false.
      I am the true and glorious God,
      but you have rejected me
          to worship idols.
12   Tell the heavens
          to tremble with fear!

13   You, my people, have sinned
          in two ways —
      you have rejected me, the source
          of life-giving water,
      and you've tried to collect water
      in cracked and leaking pits
          dug in the ground.

Ezekiel 27.1-36
God Has Destroyed the Ships
of the Seafaring City of Tyre

True North: Here is a funeral song that would have struck terror in an ancient seafaring merchant's heart. God had focused an eye on the sea peoples of Tyre, because God knew they had too much pride in their ships and their prosperous port. God asked Ezekiel, the prophet, to sing about their arrogance, for that is what had gotten Tyre into trouble. Disaster followed. We human creatures are just not that impressive to the Creator. Thank God for mercy! See also Isaiah 23.1-10; 17.12.

27 The Lord said:

^{2} Ezekiel, son of man, sing a funeral song for Tyre, ^{3} the city that is built along the sea and that trades with nations along the coast. Tell the people of Tyre that the following message is from me:

Tyre, you brag about
your perfect beauty,
^{4} and your control of the sea.

You are a ship
            built to perfection.
^{5} Builders used cypress trees
from Mount Hermon
            to make your planks
and a cedar tree from Lebanon
            for your tall mast.
^{6} Oak trees from Bashan
            were shaped into oars;
pine trees from Cyprus
            were cut for your deck,
which was then decorated
            with strips of ivory.
^{7} The builders used fancy linen
from Egypt for your sails,
            so everyone could see you.
Blue and purple cloth

from Cyprus was used
            to shade your deck.
8   Men from Sidon and Arvad
            did the rowing,
    and your own skilled workers
            were the captains.
9   Experienced men from Byblos
            repaired any damages.
    Sailors from all over
    shopped at the stores
            in your port.

10   Brave soldiers from Persia,
    Lydia, and Libya
            served in your navy,
    protecting you with shields
    and helmets,
            and making you famous.
11   Your guards came from
            Arvad and Cilicia,
    and men from Gamad
            stood watch in your towers.
    With their weapons
    hung on your walls,
            your beauty was complete.

12 Merchants from southern Spain traded silver, iron, tin, and
lead for your products. 13 The people of Greece, Tubal, and Meshech
traded slaves and things made of bronze, 14 and those from Beth-
Togarmah traded work horses, war horses, and mules. 15 You also did
business with people from Rhodes, and people from nations along the
coast gave you ivory and ebony in exchange for your goods. 16 Edom
traded emeralds, purple cloth, embroidery, fine linen, coral, and
rubies. 17 Judah and Israel gave you their finest wheat, fancy figs,
honey, olive oil, and spices in exchange for your merchandise. 18 The
people of Damascus saw what you had to offer and brought you wine
from Helbon and wool from Zahar. 19 Vedan and Javan near Uzal
traded you iron and spices. 20 The people of Dedan supplied you with
saddle blankets, 21 while people from Arabia and the rulers of Kedar

traded lambs, sheep, and goats. [22] Merchants from Sheba and Raamah gave you excellent spices, precious stones, and gold in exchange for your products. [23] You also did business with merchants from the cities of Haran, Canneh, Eden, Sheba, Asshur, and Chilmad, [24] and they gave you expensive clothing, purple and embroidered cloth, brightly colored rugs, and strong rope. [25] Large, seagoing ships carried your goods wherever they needed to go.

[26]
> You were like a ship
> loaded with heavy cargo
>> and sailing across the sea,
> but you were wrecked
>> by strong eastern winds.

[27]
> Everything on board was lost —
>> your valuable cargo,
>> your sailors and carpenters,
>> merchants and soldiers.

[28]
> The shouts of your drowning crew
>> were heard on the shore.

[29]
> Every ship is deserted;
> rowers and sailors and captains
>> all stand on shore,

30   mourning for you.
      They show their sorrow
      by putting dust on their heads
              and rolling in ashes;
31   they shave their heads
      and dress in sackcloth
              as they cry in despair.
32   In their grief they sing
              a funeral song for you:
      "Tyre, you were greater
              than all other cities.
      But now you lie in silence
              at the bottom of the sea.

33   "Nations that received
      your merchandise
              were always pleased;
      kings everywhere got rich
              from your costly goods.
34   But now you are wrecked
              in the deep sea,
      with your cargo and crew
              scattered everywhere.
35   People living along the coast
              are shocked at the news.
      Their rulers are horrified,
      and terror is written
              across their faces.
36   The merchants of the world
              can't believe what happened.
      Your death was gruesome,
              and you are gone forever."

Micah 7.18-20
The Lord God Casts our Sins into the Sea's Depths

True North: Only God can put your sins as far away as the depths of the sea you sail over, and cover them over with water to bury them forever. Christian baptism represents this burying of our sinfulness. When we are raised from the waters of baptism, we are raised to a new life in Christ; dead to sin and alive to God. So, praise God when you feel forgiven!

[The people said:]

18   Our God, no one is like you.
        We are all that is left
                of your chosen people,
        and you freely forgive
                our sin and guilt.
        You don't stay angry forever;
        you're glad to have pity
19   and pleased to be merciful.
        You will trample on our sins
                and throw them in the sea.
20   You will keep your word
        and be faithful to Jacob
                and to Abraham,
        as you promised our ancestors
                many years ago.

Habakkuk 1.12-2.14
Lord God, How Long Will We be Like Fish Trapped in a Net?

True North: What if you need God to pay attention to the evils around you? Can you be direct with God? The prophet Habakkuk spoke his complaint forcefully. God answered him. The Holy One told him that the greedy were doomed and those who honor God will fill the land like water fills the sea.

12   Holy Lord God, mighty rock,
        you are eternal,

and we are safe from death.
You are using those Babylonians
    to judge and punish others.
13 But you can't stand sin or wrong.
So don't sit by in silence
    while they gobble down people
who are better than they are.

14 The people you put on this earth
are like fish or reptiles
    without a leader.
15 Then an enemy comes along
and takes them captive
    with hooks and nets.
It makes him so happy
16 that he offers sacrifices
    to his fishing nets,
because they make him rich
    and provide choice foods.
17 Will he keep hauling in his nets
and destroying nations
    without showing mercy?

2 While standing guard
    on the watchtower,
I waited for the Lord's answer,
    before explaining the reason
    for my complaint.
2 Then the Lord told me:
"I will give you my message
    in the form of a vision.
Write it clearly enough
    to be read at a glance.
3 At the time I have decided,
    my words will come true.
You can trust what I say
    about the future.
It may take a long time,

but keep on waiting —
　　　　it will happen!

4　"I, the Lord, refuse to accept
　　　　anyone who is proud.
　Only those who live by faith
　　　　are acceptable to me."

5　Wine is treacherous,
　and arrogant people
　　　　are never satisfied.
　They are no less greedy
　　　　than death itself —
　they open their mouths as wide
　as the world of the dead
　　　　and swallow everyone.

6　But they will be mocked
　with these words:
　　　　You're doomed!
　You stored up stolen goods
　and cheated others
　　　　of what belonged to them.
7　But without warning,
　those you owe
　　　　will demand payment.
　Then you will become
　　　　a frightened victim.
8　You robbed cities and nations
　everywhere on earth
　　　　and murdered their people.
　Now those who survived
　　　　will be as cruel to you.

9　You're doomed!
　You made your family rich
　　　　at the expense of others.
　You even said to yourself,

"I'm above the law."

¹⁰ But you will bring shame
  on your family
and ruin to yourself
  for what you did to others.
¹¹ The very stones and wood
in your home
  will testify against you.

¹² You're doomed! You built a city
  on crime and violence.
¹³ But the Lord All-Powerful
  sends up in flames
what nations and people
  work so hard to gain.

¹⁴ Just as water fills the sea,
  the land will be filled
with people who know
  and honor the Lord.

SEA READINGS FROM THE OLD TESTAMENT

Seafarers and Those by Rivers Who Witnessed for God

Exodus 1.21b-2.10
When Moses was a Baby,
He was Saved From Death in a River

True North: Amazing rescues are the work of God. The daughter of Pharaoh rescued Moses from the River Nile. He was the very person whom God would choose to cause Pharaoh to lose his slaves and his armies in a mighty sea. Moses' action gave Israel the freedom to worship God without fear. In the Gospels, Jesus' followers understood him to be the same kind of liberator as Moses. Please have confidence that God desires through Jesus Christ to free you to worship God without fear. God will do it, too!

The Hebrews kept increasing [22] until finally, the king gave a command to everyone in the nation, "As soon as a Hebrew boy is born, throw him into the Nile River! But you can let the girls live."

2 A man from the Levi tribe married a woman from the same tribe, [2] and she later had a baby boy. He was a beautiful child, and she kept him inside for three months. [3] But when she could no longer keep him hidden, she made a basket out of reeds and covered it with tar. She put him in the basket and placed it in the tall grass along the edge of the Nile River. [4] The baby's older sister stood off at a distance to see what would happen to him.

[5] About that time one of the king's daughters came down to take a bath in the river, while her servant women walked along the river bank. She saw the basket in the tall grass and sent one of the young women to pull it out of the water. [6] When the king's daughter opened the basket, she saw the baby and felt sorry for him because he was crying. She said, "This must be one of the Hebrew babies."

[7] At once the baby's older sister came up and asked, "Do you want me to get a Hebrew woman to take care of the baby for you?"

[8] "Yes," the king's daughter answered.

So the girl brought the baby's mother, [9] and the king's daughter told her, "Take care of this child, and I will pay you."

The baby's mother carried him home and took care of him. [10] And when he was old enough, she took him to the king's daughter, who adopted him. She named him Moses because she said, "I pulled him out of the water."

2 Kings 2.6-14
The Prophets Elijah and Elisha Parted the Jordan River

True North: Elijah, the mighty prophet, ascended into heaven without tasting death. In the Gospels, John the Baptist's coming is described as like Elijah reappearing again. His disciple, Elisha the prophet, was able to part the Jordan river. When God does a good thing, the Holy One uses the pattern of that goodness more than once. You may see believers around you with special gifts. Some will prophesy like Elijah or John the Baptist. Some will do miracles with water like Elisha did. Some will suffer obediently like Christ did. Your own shipmates, chaplains and ship's visitors may be the people who are representing God and Jesus to you at this very moment. Keep an eye out for them!

⁶ Elijah then said to Elisha, "Now the Lord wants me to go to the Jordan River, but you must stay here."

Elisha replied, "I swear by the living Lord and by your own life that I will never leave you!" So the two of them walked on together.

⁷ Fifty prophets followed Elijah and Elisha from Jericho, then stood at a distance and watched as the two men walked toward the river. ⁸ When they got there, Elijah took off his coat, then he rolled it up and struck the water with it. At once a path opened up through the river, and the two of them walked across on dry ground.

⁹ After they had reached the other side, Elijah said, "Elisha, the Lord will soon take me away. What can I do for you before that happens?"

Elisha answered, "Please give me twice as much of your power as you give the other prophets, so I can be the one who takes your place as their leader."

¹⁰ "It won't be easy," Elijah answered. "It can happen only if you see me as I am being taken away."

¹¹ Elijah and Elisha were walking along and talking, when suddenly there appeared between them a flaming chariot pulled by fiery horses. Right away, a strong wind took Elijah up into heaven. ¹² Elisha saw this and shouted, "Israel's cavalry and chariots have taken my master away!" After Elijah had gone, Elisha tore his clothes in sorrow.

¹³ Elijah's coat had fallen off, so Elisha picked it up and walked back to the Jordan River. ¹⁴ He struck the water with the coat and

wondered, "Will the Lord perform miracles for me as he did for Elijah?" As soon as Elisha did this, a dry path opened up through the water, and he walked across.

SEA READINGS FROM THE OLD TESTAMENT

Seafarers and Those by Rivers
Who Witnessed for God

Jonah, the Reluctant, Seagoing Prophet

Seafarers have a central role in this story. They had agreed to take Jonah from Joppa to Spain. Instead, they got caught in a stormy dispute between God and Jonah. Jonah did not want to obey God by becoming a prophet and offering repentance to his nation's enemies. In the midst of the terrifying storm, the seafarers began to worship the one God as more powerful than their own. Jonah unexpectedly found salvation through facing the fate that seafarers most fear: drowning to death in the watery deep.

Jonah 1.1-16
God Desired a Prophet.
The Prophet did not Desire God.
The Seafarers Feared but Found Faith.

True North: Here is a summary of what Jonah learned. Can you flee from God when God wants you as a witness? Yes. Will it be successful? No. Will you trouble others while you flee? Yes. Will others, even believers in other gods, call you to account for your flight? Yes. Might others pray to the one God as a result? Yes. Would the seafarers' conversion have anything to do with your witness? No. God did it despite you. Will honesty before the Almighty and other seafarers make you willing to witness in foreign places? Not always, but it might make you more able to hear the Lord from the belly of your fear.

1 One day the Lord told Jonah, the son of Amittai, ² to go to the great city of Nineveh and say to the people, "The Lord has seen your terrible sins. You are doomed!"

³ Instead, Jonah ran from the Lord. He went to the seaport of Joppa and bought a ticket on a ship that was going to Spain. Then he got on the ship and sailed away to escape.

⁴ But the Lord made a strong wind blow, and such a bad storm came up that the ship was about to be broken to pieces. ⁵ The sailors were frightened, and they all started praying to their gods. They even threw the ship's cargo overboard to make the ship lighter.

All this time, Jonah was down below deck, sound asleep. ⁶ The ship's captain went to him and said, "How can you sleep at a time like this? Get up and pray to your God! Maybe he will have pity on us and keep us from drowning."

⁷ Finally, the sailors got together and said, "Let's ask our gods to show us who caused all this trouble." It turned out to be Jonah.

[8] They started asking him, "Are you the one who brought all this trouble on us? What business are you in? Where do you come from? What is your country? Who are your people?"

[9] Jonah answered, "I'm a Hebrew, and I worship the Lord God of heaven, who made the sea and the dry land."

[10] When the sailors heard this, they were frightened, because Jonah had already told them he was running from the Lord. Then they said, "Do you know what you have done?"

[11] The storm kept getting worse, until finally the sailors asked him, "What should we do with you to make the sea calm down?"

[12] Jonah told them, "Throw me into the sea, and it will calm down. I'm the cause of this terrible storm."

[13] The sailors tried their best to row to the shore. But they could not do it, and the storm kept getting worse every minute. [14] So they prayed to the Lord, "Please don't let us drown for taking this man's life. Don't hold us guilty for killing an innocent man. All of this happened because you wanted it to." [15] Then they threw Jonah overboard, and the sea calmed down. [16] The sailors were so terrified that they offered a sacrifice to the Lord and made all kinds of promises.

Jonah 1.17 to 2.1-10
Swallowed by a Great Fish and the Deep Sea

True North: You might think Jonah felt safe when he was protected from drowning in the great fish's body. He didn't. He was still afraid of dying. Jonah was right. There is no hiding from death. Vanity about our own lives and our own national interests brings no safety and will not save us. Jonah finally did remember that deliverance came from God. Jonah prayed and recovered his commitment to God. We owe loyalty also to the God who loves us and asks us to be witnesses. We, like Jonah, can be spewed up from fear of witnessing and fear of death to life.

[17] The Lord sent a big fish to swallow Jonah, and Jonah was inside the fish for three days and three nights.

2 From inside the fish, Jonah prayed to the Lord his God:
[2]   When I was in trouble, Lord,

I prayed to you,
       and you listened to me.
From deep in the world
       of the dead,
I begged for your help,
       and you answered my prayer.

3   You threw me down
       to the bottom of the sea.
The water was churning
       all around;
I was completely covered
       by your mighty waves.
4   I thought I was swept away
       from your sight,
never again to see
       your holy temple.

5   I was almost drowned
by the swirling waters
       that surrounded me.
Seaweed had wrapped
       around my head.
6   I had sunk down below
       the underwater mountains;
I knew that forever,
       I would be a prisoner there.

But, you, Lord God,
       rescued me from that pit.
7   When my life was slipping away,
       I remembered you —
and in your holy temple
       you heard my prayer.

8   All who worship worthless idols
turn from the God
       who offers them mercy.

⁹ But with shouts of praise,
I will offer a sacrifice
      to you, my Lord.
I will keep my promise,
because you are the one
      with power to save.

¹⁰ The Lord commanded the fish to vomit up Jonah on the shore. And it did.

Jonah 3.1-10
Jonah Finally did What the Lord First Asked

True North: The Ninevites were willing to respond to God's call and repent just like the sailors were. Jonah was obedient, but doubtful. Again, the mission was God's to complete. God will complete a good work in you too!

3 Once again the Lord told Jonah ² to go to that great city of Nineveh and preach his message of doom.

³ Jonah obeyed the Lord and went to Nineveh. The city was so big that it took three days just to walk through it. ⁴ After walking for a day, Jonah warned the people, "Forty days from now, Nineveh will be destroyed!"

⁵ They believed God's message and set a time when they would go without eating to show their sorrow. Then everyone in the city, no matter who they were, dressed in sackcloth.

⁶ When the king of Nineveh heard what was happening, he also dressed in sackcloth; he left the royal palace and sat in dust. ⁷⁻⁹ Then he and his officials sent out an order for everyone in the city to obey. It said:

None of you or your animals may eat or drink a thing. Each of you must wear sackcloth, and you must even put sackcloth on your animals.

You must also pray to the Lord God with all your heart and stop being sinful and cruel. Maybe God will change his mind and have mercy on us, so we won't be destroyed.

¹⁰ When God saw that the people had stopped doing evil things, he had pity and did not destroy them as he had planned.

Jonah 4.1-10
A Truly Grumpy Prophet

True North: All was well in Ninevah. But Jonah, who had been so scared of dying before, was now so angry he said it wasn't worth living any longer. Jonah's fury is why God asks us to pray for our enemies daily, asking that they be blessed by God. Otherwise, when they repent, we are still stuck in our anger. Then envy raises its head. Should God not want the repentance and restoration of everyone? Yes. Should God not want to have you be part of that good news? Most certainly, yes.

4 Jonah was really upset and angry. ² So he prayed:

Our Lord, I knew from the very beginning that you wouldn't destroy Nineveh. That's why I left my own country and headed for Spain. You are a kind and merciful God, and you are very patient. You always show love, and you don't like to punish anyone, not even foreigners.

³ Now let me die! I'd be better off dead.

⁴ The Lord replied, "What right do you have to be angry?"

⁵ Jonah then left through the east gate of the city and made a shelter to protect himself from the sun. He sat under the shelter, waiting to see what would happen to Nineveh.

⁶ The Lord made a vine grow up to shade Jonah's head and protect him from the sun. Jonah was very happy to have the vine, ⁷ but early the next morning the Lord sent a worm to chew on the vine, and the vine dried up. ⁸ During the day the Lord sent a scorching wind, and the sun beat down on Jonah's head, making him feel faint. Jonah was ready to die, and he shouted, "I wish I were dead!"

⁹ But the Lord asked, "Jonah, do you have the right to be angry about the vine?"

"Yes, I do," he answered, "and I'm angry enough to die."

¹⁰ But the Lord said:

You are concerned about a vine that you did not plant or take care of, a vine that grew up in one night and died the next. ¹¹ In that city of Nineveh there are more than a hundred twenty thousand people who cannot tell right from wrong, and many cattle are also there. Don't you think I should be concerned about that big city?

SEA READINGS FROM THE OLD TESTAMENT

Old Testament Guidance
for the People of the Sea

Exodus 20.1-17
Don't Make Idols of Anything
In or Under the Earth's Water

True North: You might think of these Ten Commandments as if they were the "Ten Regulations" given to Israel from God, the Good and Kind Captain, when they signed on as God's crew. They already knew the Captain was trustworthy for God had steered them safely across the Red Sea and out of Egypt. These regulations are useful to you in the same way they were to Israel. They give you a way to make practical and visible your trust in God. Doing these regulations does not lead any of us to think we could ever do the Captain's job. However, doing them does give honor to God and makes a ship full of human beings a safer place to be.

20 God said to the people of Israel:

² I am the Lord your God, the one who brought you out of Egypt where you were slaves.

³ Do not worship any god except me.

⁴ Do not make idols that look like anything in the sky or on earth or in the ocean under the earth. ⁵ Don't bow down and worship idols. I am the Lord your God, and I demand all your love. If you reject me, I will punish your families for three or four generations. ⁶ But if you love me and obey my laws, I will be kind to your families for thousands of generations.

⁷ Do not misuse my name. I am the Lord your God, and I will punish anyone who misuses my name.

⁸ Remember that the Sabbath Day belongs to me. ⁹ You have six days when you can do your work, ¹⁰ but the seventh day of each week belongs to me, your God. No one is to work on that day — not you, your children, your slaves, your animals, or the foreigners who live in your towns. ¹¹ In six days I made the sky, the earth, the oceans, and everything in them, but on the seventh day I rested. That's why I made the Sabbath a special day that belongs to me.

¹² Respect your father and your mother, and you will live a long time in the land I am giving you.

¹³ Do not murder.

¹⁴ Be faithful in marriage.

¹⁵ Do not steal.

¹⁶ Do not tell lies about others.

¹⁷ Do not want anything that belongs to someone else. Don't want anyone's house, wife or husband, slaves, oxen, donkeys or anything else.

Leviticus 11.9-19
Don't Eat Anything in the Water
That has No Fins or Scales

True North: Israel received from God through Moses many regulations concerning food to help the people keep in a proper relationship with God. As you know from shipboard life, impure food and polluted water bring illness and danger to everyone. God provided the following regulations to help seafarers. From creatures of the water, they were to catch for eating only those fish with fins and scales (9-12). From water birds, they were not to catch or eat anything that ate its own kind, ate dead creatures, or ate meat (13-19). These regulations remain to this day among many Jews. How does having boundaries help you? Read Mark 7.14-23 in the section, "New Testament Guidance for the People of the Sea" to learn how Jesus reinterpreted these rules about eating food.

11 The Lord told Moses and Aaron ² to say to the community of Israel:

⁹₋¹² You may eat anything that lives in water and has fins and scales. But it would be disgusting for you to eat anything else that lives in water, and you must not even touch their dead bodies.

¹³₋¹⁹ Eagles, vultures, buzzards, crows, ostriches, hawks, sea gulls, owls, pelicans, storks, herons, hoopoes, and bats are also disgusting, and you are forbidden to eat any of them.

Deuteronomy 4.15-20
Do Not Make Idols out of Fish

True North: Our Creator chose to be revealed through fire and smoke so as to make it hard to see God. God chose to do this so we would not take a physical image of God or the physical image of the Creator's gifts, and make them into an idol that we would slave to satisfy. For idols will snare you, not lead you to a life of freedom. We make idols from the best God has given, such as families, productive labor and even money. Idolatry happens when we strive like slaves to please our families or our captains or to get more money than anyone else. Then we are no longer giving our attention to what God is doing. For more about the dangers of idolatry, read Romans 1.18-25.

[Moses said to Israel:]
   [15] When God spoke to you from the fire, he was invisible. So be careful [16] not to commit the sin of worshiping idols. Don't make idols to be worshiped, whether they are shaped like men, women, [17] animals, birds, [18] reptiles, or fish. [19] And when you see the sun or moon or stars, don't be tempted to bow down and worship them. The Lord put them there for all the other nations to worship. [20] But you are the Lord's people, because he led you through fiery trials and rescued you from Egypt.

Job 28.12-28
Wisdom was with God when
God Divided the Waters at Creation

True North: Wisdom comes upon you when you respect our most amazing God. It cannot be bought from people. It is God's free gift to you when you stand in awe of your Creator.

[12]   But where is wisdom found?
[13]   No human knows the way.
[14]   Nor can it be discovered
             in the deepest sea.
[15]   It is worth much more
         than silver or pure gold
[16]   or precious stones.
[17]   Nothing is its equal —
             not gold or costly glass.
[18]   Wisdom is worth much more than
             coral, jasper, or rubies.

19 All the topaz of Ethiopia
and the finest gold
cannot compare with it.
20 Where then is wisdom?
21 It is hidden from human eyes
and even from birds.
22 Death and destruction
have merely heard rumors
about where it is found.
23 God is the only one who knows
the way to wisdom,
24 because he sees everything
beneath the heavens.
25 When God divided out
the wind and the water,
26 and when he decided the path
for rain and lightning,
27 he also determined the truth
and defined wisdom.
28 God told us, "Wisdom means
that you respect me, the Lord,
and turn from sin."

Proverbs 8.22-36
Wisdom was There when God Established the Deep Seas

True North: Wisdom worked like a shipwright next to God. Wisdom delights in you and would help you on your way. Share these verses with some one who is feeling unwanted and unworthy.

22 From the beginning,
I was with the Lord.
I was there before he began
23 to create the earth.
At the very first,
the Lord gave life to me.

24 When I was born,
there were no oceans
or springs of water.
25 My birth was before
mountains were formed
or hills were put in place.
26 It happened long before God
had made the earth
or any of its fields
or even the dust.

27 I was there when the Lord
put the heavens in place
and stretched the sky
over the surface of the sea.
28 I was with him when he placed
the clouds in the sky
and created the springs
that fill the ocean.
29 I was there when he set
boundaries for the sea
to make it obey him,
and when he laid foundations
to support the earth.

30 I was right beside the Lord,
helping him plan and build.
I made him happy each day,
and I was happy at his side.
31 I was pleased with his world
and pleased with its people.

32 Pay attention, my children!
Follow my advice,
and you will be happy.
33 Listen carefully
to my instructions,
and you will be wise.

34 Come to my home each day
and listen to me.
You will find happiness.
35 By finding me, you find life,
and the Lord will be pleased
with you.
36 But if you don't find me,
you hurt only yourself,
and if you hate me,
you are in love with death.

Four Sayings from Proverbs:
Watch what you Spill and what you Drink

True North: Proverbs is a book of wisdom sayings. Each saying is separated from the next one by a double space. The ones that talk about water concern family life, arguments and drinking problems.

Proverbs 17.14

14 The start of an argument
is like a water leak —
so stop it before
real trouble breaks out.

Proverbs 23.15-35

15 My children,
if you show good sense,
I will be happy,
16 and if you are truthful,
I will really be glad.

17 Don't be jealous of sinners,
but always honor the Lord.
18 Then you will truly have hope
for the future.

19   Listen to me, my children!
     Be wise and have enough sense
               to follow the right path.
20   Don't be a heavy drinker
               or stuff yourself with food.
21   It will make you feel drowsy,
     and you will end up poor
               with only rags to wear.

22   Pay attention to your father,
     and don't neglect your mother
               when she grows old.
23   Invest in truth and wisdom,
     discipline and good sense,
               and don't part with them.
24   Make your father truly happy
     by living right and showing
               sound judgment.

25   Make your parents proud,
               especially your mother.

26   My son, pay close attention,
      and gladly follow
               my example.
27   Bad women and unfaithful wives
               are like a deep pit —
28   they are waiting to attack you
      like a gang of robbers
               with victim after victim.

29   Who is always in trouble?
               Who argues and fights?
      Who has cuts and bruises?
               Whose eyes are red?
30   Everyone who stays up late,
               having just one more drink.

31   Don't even look
      at that colorful stuff
               bubbling up in the glass!
      It goes down so easily,
32   but later it bites
               like a poisonous snake.
33   You will see weird things,
      and your mind
               will play tricks on you.
34   You will feel tossed about
      like someone trying to sleep
               on a ship in a storm.
35   You will be bruised all over,
      without even remembering
               how it all happened.
      And you will lie awake asking,
      "When will morning come,
               so I can drink some more?"

Proverbs 25.25

25 Good news from far away
    refreshes like cold water
        when you are thirsty.

Proverbs 31.4-9

4 Kings and leaders
   should not get drunk
       or even want to drink.
5 Drinking makes you forget
   your responsibilities,
       and you mistreat the poor.
6 Beer and wine are only
   for the dying or for those
       who have lost all hope.
7 Let them drink and forget
   how poor and miserable
       they feel.
8 But you must defend
   those who are helpless
       and have no hope.
9 Be fair and give justice
   to the poor and homeless.

Proverbs 31.10-31
Advice from King Lemuel's Mother

True North: The virtues in this passage apply to whichever seafarer's or fisher's spouse stays home. When you are at sea, think of your spouse as provisioning your family like a banana boat provisions the world's families.

10 A truly good wife
    is the most precious treasure
        a man can find!
11 Her husband depends on her,
    and she never
        lets him down.

12 She is good to him
       every day of her life,
13 and with her own hands
       she gladly makes clothes.
14 She is like a sailing ship
   that brings food
       from across the sea.
15 She gets up before daylight
   to prepare food for her family
       and for her servants.
16 She knows how to buy land
   and how to plant a vineyard,
17   and she always works hard.
18 She knows when to buy or sell,
   and she stays busy
       until late at night.
19 She spins her own cloth,
20 and she helps the poor
       and the needy.
21 Her family has warm clothing,
   and so she doesn't worry
       when it snows.
22 She does her own sewing,
   and everything she wears
       is beautiful.

23 Her husband is a well-known
   and respected leader
       in the city.
24 She makes clothes to sell
       to the shop owners.
25 She is strong and graceful,
   as well as cheerful
       about the future.
26 Her words are sensible,
   and her advice
       is thoughtful.
27 She takes good care

of her family
and is never lazy.
28 Her children praise her,
and with great pride
her husband says,
29 "There are many good women,
but you are the best!"

30 Charm can be deceiving,
and beauty fades away,
but a woman
who honors the Lord
deserves to be praised.
31 Show her respect —
praise her in public
for what she has done.

Ecclesiastes 9.7-12
Trapped Like a Fish in a Net

True North: *God wants your life to be happy. Do not wear yourself down with worry over loneliness or loss. You can't escape these things or predict them. But God does not chose to bring calamity upon believers. The world does that on its own. When sorrow comes upon you, take courage from Jesus' resurrection to eternal life. It shows how much God will do for you in this life and the next. At the end of time, you will meet your Lord and never be separate from him again. So rejoice as you can where you can, even at work far at sea. See 1 Thessalonians 4:13-18 for a happy view of meeting Jesus at the end time in the section Sea Readings About God's Eternal Reign.*

7 Be happy and enjoy eating and drinking! God decided long ago that this is what you should do. 8 Dress up, comb your hair, and look your best. 9 Life is short, and you love your wife, so enjoy being with her. This is what you are supposed to do as you struggle through life on this earth. 10 Work hard at whatever you do. You will soon go to the world of the dead, where no one works or thinks or reasons or knows anything.

[11] Here is something else I have learned:
The fastest runners
        and the greatest heroes
don't always win races
        and battles.
Wisdom, intelligence, and skill
don't always make you healthy,
        rich, or popular.
We each have our share
        of bad luck.
[12] None of us know when we might fall victim to a sudden disaster and find ourselves like fish in a net or birds in a trap.

Ecclesiastes 11:1-2
Send Out Your Bread on the Water
And it Will Come Back

True North: This verse is a difficult one to translate from the Hebrew language. It literally means "Send out your bread upon the water." It may refer to trading ships carrying grain. If you put all your grain in one ship, you risk much more than if you put the grain in several ships. Only the first of the two translations below uses the "bread on the waters" language. So, don't put all your oil in one tanker! Or all your hope in one set of sailing papers, or in one translation of scripture!

[1] Send out your bread upon the waters, for after many days you will get it back. [2] Divide your means seven ways, or even eight, for you do not know what disaster may happen on earth. (NRSV)

11   Be generous, and someday
                you will be rewarded.
[2]   Share what you have
                with seven or eight others,
        because you never know
                when disaster may strike. (CEV)

Wisdom of Solomon 5.1-14
The Righteous Will Amaze the Unrighteous

True North: This book of wisdom is associated with the Old Testament. Its comfort is to tell you how the righteous will stand confidently in the presence of their oppressors and by their confidence will bring the unrighteous to dismay. St. Paul wrote that while he was yet a Jew, he had a similar experience when he met confident joyful Christians. Their witness, while they underwent persecution from Paul, brought him to know Jesus was truly the Son of God. On board a ship where many may not believe as you do, stand confidently and joyfully in the salvation granted to you by God through Christ. It will be the unrighteous who will become dismayed and think their previous lives are worth no more than the trace of a ship's passing wake. You can read what Paul wrote about his conversion in I Corinthians 1.1-11; Galatians 1.11-18.

5:[1] Then the righteous will stand with great confidence in the presence of those who have oppressed them and those who make light of their labors. [2] When the unrighteous see them, they will be shaken with dreadful fear, and they will be amazed at the unexpected salvation of the righteous. [3] They will speak to one another in repentance, and in anguish of spirit they will groan, and say, [4] "These are persons whom we once held in derision and made a byword of reproach— fools that we were! We thought that their lives were madness and that their end was without honor. [5] Why have they been numbered among the children of God? And why is their lot among the saints? [6] So it was we who strayed from the way of truth, and the light of righteousness did not shine on us, and the sun did not rise upon us. 5:[7] We took our fill of the paths of lawlessness and destruction, and we journeyed through trackless deserts, but the way of the Lord we have not known. [8] What has our arrogance profited us? And what good has our boasted wealth brought us? [9] "All those things have vanished like a shadow, and like a rumor that passes by; [10] like a ship that sails through the billowy water, and when it has passed no trace can be found, no track of its keel in the waves; [11] or as, when a bird flies through the air, no evidence of its passage is found; the light air, lashed by the beat of its pinions and pierced by the force of its rushing flight, is traversed by the movement of its wings, and afterward no sign of its coming is found there; [12] or as, when an arrow is shot at a target, the air, thus divided, comes together at once, so that no one knows its pathway. [13] So we also, as soon as we were born, ceased to be, and we had no sign of virtue to show, but were consumed in our wickedness." [14] Because the hope of the ungodly is like thistledown carried by the wind, and like a light frost driven away by a storm; it is dispersed like smoke before the wind, and it passes like the remembrance of a guest who stays but a day. (NRSV)

Wisdom of Solomon 14.1-7
It is your Providence, O Father,
That Steers the Ship on its Path in the Sea

True North: The smallest craft that travels is observed from the Divine Mariner's bridge. The frailest seafarer who travels is observed from the Divine Mariner's bridge. Read Matthew 6:25-34 to see how Jesus described God's caring, watchful eye.

14:[1] Again, one preparing to sail and about to voyage over raging waves calls upon a piece of wood more fragile than the ship that carries him. [2] For it was desire for gain that planned that vessel, and wisdom was the artisan who built it; [3] but it is your providence, O Father, that steers its course, because you have given it a path in the sea, and a safe way through the waves, [4] showing that you can save from every danger, so that even a person who lacks skill may put to sea. [5] It is your will that works of your wisdom should not be without effect; therefore people trust their lives even to the smallest piece of wood, and passing through the billows on a raft they come safely to land. [6] For even in the beginning, when arrogant giants were perishing, the hope of the world took refuge on a raft, and guided by your hand left to the world the seed of a new generation. [7] For blessed is the wood by which righteousness comes. (NRSV)

SEA READINGS FROM THE NEW TESTAMENT
How Jesus Directed the Waters
to Save People and Make Disciples

Jesus' Power Over Water
was the Same as God's
Power Over Water

In this section and the next you will find many references to the sea around which Jesus conducted most of his mighty deeds. The Sea of Galilee was always known as a "sea," in Jewish tradition, because it was so big. In Roman times, the word 'sea' was reserved for bodies of salt water, so the Sea of Galilee became known as Lake Galilee, or Lake Gennesaret (for its lyre shape) or Lake Tiberias (for its major lakeside city). These are all the same body of water.

We have four gospels, Matthew, Mark, Luke and John. They all contain stories of Jesus' time among us. They often tell similar stories of miracles and healings. We have included one of the parallel stories when there are several. The others will be listed by reference so you can look them up.

Matthew 8.18-27
The Creator's Son Controlled
the Galilean Winds and Waves

True North: At this early point in Jesus' ministry, his disciples needed to learn that following Jesus meant they were always safe even if they had nowhere to lay their heads. He had the same control over nature that God did. In the New Testament Jesus always acted to save people. He wants to save you now. He is not a warrior Messiah, but a saving Messiah. "Messiah" is the Hebrew word for "one anointed or chosen by God". It means the same as the Greek word "Christ". Read the parallel texts in Mark 4.35-41; Luke 8.22-25.

[18] When Jesus saw the crowd, he went across Lake Galilee. [19] A teacher of the Law of Moses came up to him and said, "Teacher, I'll go anywhere with you!"

[20] Jesus replied, "Foxes have dens, and birds have nests. But the Son of Man doesn't have a place to call his own."

[21] Another disciple said to Jesus, "Lord, let me wait till I bury my father."

[22] Jesus answered, "Come with me, and let the dead bury their dead."

[23] After Jesus left in a boat with his disciples, [24] a terrible storm suddenly struck the lake, and waves started splashing into their boat.

Jesus was sound asleep, [25] so the disciples went over to him and woke him up. They said, "Lord, save us! We're going to drown!"

[26] But Jesus replied, "Why are you so afraid? You surely don't have much faith." Then he got up and ordered the wind and the waves to calm down. And everything was calm.

[27] The men in the boat were amazed and said, "Who is this? Even the wind and the waves obey him."

Matthew 14.22-34
Jesus, the Son of God,
Saved Peter from Drowning

True North: Jesus took time to pray before he walked on water. Peter would have felt more confident in those risky waters if he had prayed first. Let us pray and thank Jesus that then as today, he has made it his mission to rescue us when we call for help! His power acting for you will save you. Read also the texts in Mark 6.45-52; John 6.16-21.

[22] Right away, Jesus made his disciples get into a boat and start back across the lake. But he stayed until he had sent the crowds away. [23] Then he went up on a mountain where he could be alone and pray. Later that evening, he was still there.

[24] By this time the boat was a long way from the shore. It was going against the wind and was being tossed around by the waves. [25] A little while before morning, Jesus came walking on the water toward his disciples. [26] When they saw him, they thought he was a ghost. They were terrified and started screaming.

[27] At once, Jesus said to them, "Don't worry! I am Jesus. Don't be afraid."

[28] Peter replied, "Lord, if it is really you, tell me to come to you on the water."

[29] "Come on!" Jesus said. Peter then got out of the boat and started walking on the water toward him.

[30] But when Peter saw how strong the wind was, he was afraid and started sinking. "Save me, Lord!" he shouted.

[31] Right away, Jesus reached out his hand. He helped Peter up and said, "You surely don't have much faith. Why do you doubt?"

[32] When Jesus and Peter got into the boat, the wind died down. [33] The men in the boat worshiped Jesus and said, "You really are the Son of God!" [34] Jesus and his disciples crossed the lake and came to shore near the town of Gennesaret.

Matthew 17.24-27
Right From the Fish's Mouth

True North: Jesus didn't think of himself as a foreigner in any place in the world because he was the Son of the Creator of the world. Still he was willing to pay "port taxes" in order to reach all people, especially those who didn't know he was the Son of God. Like Jesus, believers are also children of God and free in Christ. We want to reach all people. What we give in taxes, we know came first from the Creator. We give our taxes in service to others. We also give to maritime ministries for seafarers like you through our congregations. Won't you help us support and comfort other seafarers who need good news as much as you?

[24] When Jesus and the others arrived in Capernaum, the collectors for the temple tax came to Peter and asked, "Does your teacher pay the temple tax?"

[25] "Yes, he does," Peter answered.

After they had returned home, Jesus went up to Peter and asked him, "Simon, what do you think? Do the kings of this earth collect taxes and fees from their own people or from foreigners?"

[26] Peter answered, "From foreigners."

Jesus replied, "Then their own people don't have to pay. [27] But we don't want to cause trouble. So go cast a line into the lake and pull out the first fish you hook. Open its mouth, and you will find a coin. Use it to pay your taxes and mine."

John 2.1-11
Jesus Showed His Power Over Creation
by Changing Water into a New and Better Wine

*True North: Jesus was a quiet and modest guest at this wedding. He did not make a loud witness to his powers over creation. In fact, the bridegroom got complimented for Jesus' miracle! We too should not "fog horn" the gifts God has given us as if they were our own invention. For then our actions would be signs pointing to us! We would no longer be saying, "Come and see the power of God!" So, claim God's power but name it as **God's** power.*

2 Three days later Mary, the mother of Jesus, was at a wedding feast in the village of Cana in Galilee. [2] Jesus and his disciples had also been invited and were there.

[3] When the wine was all gone, Mary said to Jesus, "They don't have any more wine."

[4] Jesus replied, "Mother, my time hasn't yet come! You must not tell me what to do."

[5] Mary then said to the servants, "Do whatever Jesus tells you to do."

[6] At the feast there were six stone water jars that were used by the people for washing themselves in the way that their religion said they must. Each jar held about twenty or thirty gallons. [7] Jesus told the servants to fill them to the top with water. Then after the jars had been filled, [8] he said, "Now take some water and give it to the man in charge of the feast."

The servants did as Jesus told them, [9] and the man in charge drank some of the water that had now turned into wine. He did not know where the wine had come from, but the servants did. He called the bridegroom over [10] and said, "The best wine is always served first. Then after the guests have had plenty, the other wine is served. But you have kept the best until last!"

[11] This was Jesus' first miracle, and he did it in the village of Cana in Galilee. There Jesus showed his glory, and his disciples put their faith in him.

How Jesus Directed the Waters
to Save People and Make Disciples

Jesus was God's Son and He was Greater than Noah and Jonah

Matthew 3.5-17
At Jesus' Baptism,
God Declared, "This is my Own Dear Son."

True North: Jesus began his ministry by accepting John the Baptizer's excitement that Jesus was the one who had come from God. The baptism Jesus received did not wash away any sins in him. There were none to wash away. For Jesus this baptism was the means for his receiving the Holy Spirit. This Holy Spirit was a parent and guide for him throughout his whole ministry. In baptism Christians have both experiences: a washing away of our sins and our commissioning as beloved spirit-begotten children of God. Read the parallel texts at Mark 1.1-11; Luke 3.1-9, 16-17.

[5] From Jerusalem and all Judea and from the Jordan River Valley crowds of people went to John. [6] They told how sorry they were for their sins, and he baptized them in the river.

[7] Many Pharisees and Sadducees also came to be baptized. But John said to them:

You bunch of snakes! Who warned you to run from the coming judgment? [8] Do something to show that you have really given up your sins. [9] And don't start telling yourselves that you belong to Abraham's family. I tell you that God can turn these stones into children for Abraham. [10] An ax is ready to cut the trees down at their roots. Any tree that doesn't produce good fruit will be chopped down and thrown into a fire.

[11] I baptize you with water so that you will give up your sins. But someone more powerful is going to come, and I am not good enough even to carry his sandals. He will baptize you with the Holy Spirit and with fire. [12] His threshing fork is in his hand, and he is ready to separate the wheat from the husks. He will store the wheat in a barn and burn the husks in a fire that never goes out.

The Baptism of Jesus

[13] Jesus left Galilee and went to the Jordan River to be baptized by John. [14] But John kept objecting and said, "I ought to be baptized by you. Why have you come to me?"

[15] Jesus answered, "For now this is how it should be, because we must do all that God wants us to do." Then John agreed.

[16] So Jesus was baptized. And as soon as he came out of the water, the sky opened, and he saw the Spirit of God coming down on him like a dove. [17] Then a voice from heaven said, "This is my own dear Son, and I am pleased with him."

Luke 3.23-38
Jesus was Greater than Noah,
Even Though Noah Saved His Believing Family
from the Worst Flood Ever

True North: So many names! Only a few are really important for seafarers and fishers to know although you may find your own name in this list. Jesus was a son of the lineage of David, the faithful king. Jesus was a son of Abraham, the trusting, adventuring patriarch who risked his son for God. Jesus was a son of Noah, the shipwright and seafarer who saved the world by God's command. Jesus was a son of Adam, everyone's ancestor, and he was the Son of God. Through Jesus, these are all your ancestors as are the faithful women who gave birth to all these believers.

[23] When Jesus began to preach, he was about thirty years old. Everyone thought he was the son of Joseph. But his family went back through Heli, [24] Matthat, Levi, Melchi, Jannai, Joseph, [25] Mattathias, Amos, Nahum, Esli, Naggai, [26] Maath, Mattathias, Semein, Josech, Joda;

[27] Joanan, Rhesa, Zerubbabel, Shealtiel, Neri, [28] Melchi, Addi, Cosam, Elmadam, Er, [29] Joshua, Eliezer, Jorim, Matthat, Levi;

[30] Simeon, Judah, Joseph, Jonam, Eliakim, [31] Melea, Menna, Mattatha, Nathan, David, [32] Jesse, Obed, Boaz, Salmon, Nahshon;

[33] Amminadab, Admin, Arni, Hezron, Perez, Judah, [34] Jacob, Isaac, Abraham, Terah, Nahor, [35] Serug, Reu, Peleg, Eber, Shelah;

[36] Cainan, Arphaxad, Shem, Noah, Lamech, [37] Methuselah, Enoch, Jared, Mahalaleel, Kenan, [38] Enosh, and Seth.

The family of Jesus went all the way back to Adam and then to God.

Matthew 24.37-39
When Jesus, the Son of Man, Appeared,
It was Like Reliving the Days of Noah and the Flood

True North: Why is Jesus called a descendent of Noah? Because the times of Jesus were once again as close to human disaster as were the times of Noah. As Noah was called to faithfully rescue his family, so too was Jesus called to rescue the family of God. Jesus proclaimed, "The time has come. God's kingdom will soon be here." We who believe know that the kingdom came fully through Jesus' death and resurrection. The Son of Man is someone God mercifully sends from heaven in the form of a human being when great chaos threatens. Read also the parallel, Luke 17.26-27.

Jesus said:

[37] When the Son of Man appears, things will be just as they were when Noah lived. [38] People were eating, drinking, and getting married right up to the day that the flood came and Noah went into the big boat. [39] They didn't know anything was happening until the flood came and swept them all away. That is how it will be when the Son of Man appears.

Matthew 12.38-42
Jesus, the Son of Man, was Greater than Jonah

True North: Jesus described Jonah's three days of near-death in the great fish as parallel to Jesus' three days of death in the tomb. As Jonah was rescued by God, so would Jesus be rescued by God. Jesus was not about to do fancy signs in the heavens, signs to impress ministers and priests. Instead, he showed God's power to save people. He can do the same saving for you. Read also Matthew 16.4; Luke 11.29-32.

[38] Some Pharisees and teachers of the Law of Moses said, "Teacher, we want you to show us a sign from heaven."

[39] But Jesus replied:

You want a sign because you are evil and won't believe! But the only sign you will get is the sign of the prophet Jonah. [40] He was in the stomach of a big fish for three days and nights, just as the Son of

Man will be deep in the earth for three days and nights. [41] On the day of judgment the people of Nineveh will stand there with you and condemn you. They turned to God when Jonah preached, and yet here is something far greater than Jonah. [42] The Queen of the South will also stand there with you and condemn you. She traveled a long way to hear Solomon's wisdom, and yet here is something much greater than Solomon.

Matthew 11.18-30
Some Cities WhereJesus Preached and did Miracles Were more Unkind to Jesus than the Sea Merchant City Tyre was to its Neighbors

True North: Even while warning these cities, Jesus made it very clear by his prayer that what he wanted most was to lift the burdens of their citizens and give them peace and rest. He wants to do the same for you! Read also the parallel at Luke 10.13-15, 21-22.

Jesus said to the crowds:

[18] John the Baptist did not go around eating and drinking, and you said, "That man has a demon in him!" [19] But the Son of Man goes around eating and drinking, and you say, "That man eats and drinks too much! He is even a friend of tax collectors and sinners." Yet Wisdom is shown to be right by what it does.

[20] In the towns where Jesus had worked most of his miracles, the people refused to turn to God. So Jesus was upset with them and said:

[21] You people of Chorazin are in for trouble! You people of Bethsaida are in for trouble too! If the miracles that took place in your towns had happened in Tyre and Sidon, the people there would have turned to God long ago. They would have dressed in sackcloth and put ashes on their heads. [22] I tell you that on the day of judgment the people of Tyre and Sidon will get off easier than you will.

[23] People of Capernaum, do you think you will be honored in heaven? You will go down to hell! If the miracles that took place in your town had happened in Sodom, that town would still be standing. [24] So I tell you that on the day of judgment the people of Sodom will get off easier than you.

Then Jesus prayed:

²⁵ At that moment Jesus said:

My Father, Lord of heaven and earth, I am grateful that you hid all this from wise and educated people and showed it to ordinary people. ²⁶ Yes, Father, that is what pleased you.

Jesus spoke again to the crowd:

²⁷ My Father has given me everything, and he is the only one who knows the Son. The only one who truly knows the Father is the Son. But the Son wants to tell others about the Father, so that they can know him too.

²⁸ If you are tired from carrying heavy burdens, come to me and I will give you rest. ²⁹ Take the yoke I give you. Put it on your shoulders and learn from me. I am gentle and humble, and you will find rest. ³⁰ This yoke is easy to bear, and this burden is light.

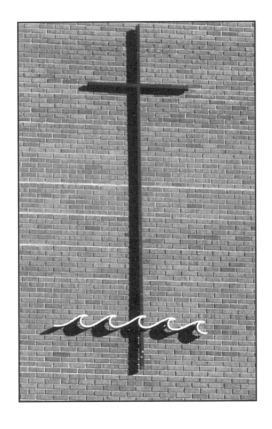

SEA READINGS FROM THE NEW TESTAMENT

How Jesus Directed the Waters
to Save People and Make Disciples

Jesus Saved by the Sea
and from Water

Mark 5.1-20
Jesus Cast out Evil Spirits
Fom a Man Driven to Despair

True North: Watch how Jesus healed a demon-possessed man. He went out of his way across the Sea of Galilee to another country to heal this foreigner. He drew near to the man who was possessed by lots of evil spirits. He listened to the story about the evil that was causing the man to try and kill himself. He asked the man's name. He sent away the evil spirits. Thanks be to Jesus who reaches out to us in our despair, learns our names, throws out the evil within us and turns the despairing into disciples! As disciples of Jesus, we too can draw near to others, ask their name, find out their pain, lay hands on them and pray to Jesus to intercede. Read also the parallels, Matthew 8.28-9.1; Luke 8.26-37. Thanks be to God for this ministry.

[5] Jesus and his disciples crossed Lake Galilee and came to shore near the town of Gerasa. [2] When he was getting out of the boat, a man with an evil spirit quickly ran to him [3] from the graveyard where he had been living. No one was able to tie the man up anymore, not even with a chain. [4] He had often been put in chains and leg irons, but he broke the chains and smashed the leg irons. No one could control him. [5] Night and day he was in the graveyard or on the hills, yelling and cutting himself with stones.

[6] When the man saw Jesus in the distance, he ran up to him and knelt down. [7] He shouted, "Jesus, Son of God in heaven, what do you want with me? Promise me in God's name that you won't torture me!" [8] The man said this because Jesus had already told the evil spirit to come out of him.

[9] Jesus asked, "What is your name?"

The man answered, "My name is Lots, because I have 'lots' of evil spirits." [10] He then begged Jesus not to send them away.

[11] Over on the hillside a large herd of pigs was feeding. [12] So the evil spirits begged Jesus, "Send us into those pigs! Let us go into them." [13] Jesus let them go, and they went out of the man and into the pigs. The whole herd of about two thousand pigs rushed down the steep bank into the lake and drowned.

[14] The men taking care of the pigs ran to the town and the farms to spread the news. Then the people came out to see what had happened. [15] When they came to Jesus, they saw the man who had once been full of

demons. He was sitting there with his clothes on and in his right mind, and they were terrified.

[16] Everyone who had seen what had happened told about the man and the pigs. [17] Then the people started begging Jesus to leave their part of the country.

[18] When Jesus was getting into the boat, the man begged to go with him. [19] But Jesus would not let him. Instead, he said, "Go home to your family and tell them how much the Lord has done for you and how good he has been to you."

[20] The man went away into the region near the ten cities known as Decapolis and began telling everyone how much Jesus had done for him. Everyone who heard what had happened was amazed.

Mark 9.17-29
Be Sure to Have Faith
When You Face the Dangers of Water or Fire

True North: In life and death situations, prayer is your anchor in God. A prayer can be short, like the disciples' prayer at sea, "Lord, Save us! We're going to drown!" (Mt 8.25) In this reading the disciples needed to pray, "Lord, help this poor child! Restore him to his right mind!" Read also the parallels in Matthew 17.14-20; Luke 9.37-43. The image of danger and rescue in this passage comes from Isaiah 43.2-3. God said, "When you cross deep waters I will be with you and you won't drown. When you walk through fire you won't be burned or scorched by flames." Let God know through prayer that you want to have this same protection at sea.

[17] Someone from the crowd answered, "Teacher, I brought my son to you. A demon keeps him from talking. [18] Whenever the demon attacks my son, it throws him to the ground and makes him foam at the mouth and grit his teeth in pain. Then he becomes stiff. I asked your disciples to force out the demon, but they couldn't do it."

[19] Jesus said, "You people don't have any faith! How much longer must I be with you? Why do I have to put up with you? Bring the boy to me."

[20] They brought the boy, and as soon as the demon saw Jesus, it made the boy shake all over. He fell down and began rolling on the ground and foaming at the mouth.

[21] Jesus asked the boy's father, "How long has he been like this?"

The man answered, "Ever since he was a child. [22] The demon has often tried to kill him by throwing him into a fire or into water. Please have pity and help us if you can!"

[23] Jesus replied, "Why do you say 'if you can'? Anything is possible for someone who has faith!"

[24] Right away the boy's father shouted, "I do have faith! Please help me to have even more."

[25] When Jesus saw that a crowd was gathering fast, he spoke sternly to the evil spirit that had kept the boy from speaking or hearing. He said, "I order you to come out of the boy! Don't ever bother him again."

[26] The spirit screamed and made the boy shake all over. Then it went out of him. The boy looked dead, and almost everyone said he was. [27] But Jesus took hold of his hand and helped him stand up.

[28] After Jesus and the disciples had gone back home and were alone, they asked him, "Why couldn't we force out that demon?"

[29] Jesus answered, "Only prayer can force out that kind of demon."

John 5.1-9
Jesus Healed a Man
Too Sick to Enter the Healing Pool

True North: Don't be afraid to ask Jesus for help. Jesus desires to heal you and teach you to stand on your own two feet.

[5] Later, Jesus went to Jerusalem for another Jewish festival. [2] In the city near the sheep gate was a pool with five porches, and its name in Hebrew was Bethzatha.

[3-4] Many sick, blind, lame, and crippled people were lying close to the pool.

⁵ Beside the pool was a man who had been sick for thirty-eight years. ⁶ When Jesus saw the man and realized that he had been crippled for a long time, he asked him, "Do you want to be healed?"

⁷ The man answered, "Lord, I don't have anyone to put me in the pool when the water is stirred up. I try to get in, but someone else always gets there first."

⁸ Jesus told him, "Pick up your mat and walk!" ⁹ Right then the man was healed. He picked up his mat and started walking around. The day on which this happened was a Sabbath.

SEA READINGS FROM THE NEW TESTAMENT

How Jesus Directed the Waters
to Save People and Make Disciples

Jesus Taught by the Sea
and about the Sea

Matthew 13.47-50
The Kingdom of Heaven is
Like Gathering Fish into Nets

True North: Most fishing on Lake Galilee was by casting nets. Jesus wanted the disciples to be like net fishers. They were to work together, as you must on a ship, and draw people together for God. Some people who were drawn in were like fish that were not good, but everyone was still wanted by God. Disciples will keep drawing people in until the end of time.

[47] The kingdom of heaven is like what happens when a net is thrown into a lake and catches all kinds of fish. [48] When the net is full, it is dragged to the shore, and the fishermen sit down to separate the fish. They keep the good ones, but throw the bad ones away. [49] That's how it will be at the end of time. Angels will come and separate the evil people from the ones who have done right. [50] Then those evil people will be thrown into a flaming furnace, where they will cry and grit their teeth in pain.

Matthew 14.13-21
By Lake Galilee, Jesus Fed
Thousands with a Fisher's Meal

True North: We have a compassionate Lord Jesus. He taught the crowd when they tracked him down. He fed them when they were hungry. Seafarers' centers and Bethel chapels are there to do the same for you when your ship arrives in port. When someone offers to pray with you, study the Bible with you, talk about problems with you, he or she is being like Jesus with you. You may be like Jesus with them, too! Read also the parallels, Mark 6.30-34; Luke 9.10-17; John 6.1-14.

[13] After Jesus heard about John, he crossed Lake Galilee to go to some place where he could be alone. But the crowds found out and followed him on foot from the towns. [14] When Jesus got out of the boat, he saw the large crowd. He felt sorry for them and healed everyone who was sick.

[15] That evening the disciples came to Jesus and said, "This place is like a desert, and it is already late. Let the crowds leave, so they can go to the villages and buy some food."

[16] Jesus replied, "They don't have to leave. Why don't you give them something to eat?"

[17] But they said, "We have only five small loaves of bread and two fish." [18] Jesus asked his disciples to bring the food to him, [19] and he told the crowd to sit down on the grass. Jesus took the five loaves and the two fish. He looked up toward heaven and blessed the food. Then he broke the bread and handed it to his disciples, and they gave it to the people.

[20] After everyone had eaten all they wanted, Jesus' disciples picked up twelve large baskets of leftovers.

[21] There were about five thousand men who ate, not counting the women and children.

SEA READINGS FROM THE NEW TESTAMENT

How Jesus Directed the Waters
to Save People and Make Disciples

Jesus Taught About
Living Water

John 3.1-21
To be Born From Above
Takes Water and the Spirit

True North: Jesus taught about water and spirit baptism as a sign of a believer's new life in God. God did not send Jesus to condemn you. If you believe that Jesus is the Son of God, you may have within you living water and a living spirit to sustain you in all worldly troubles. If you have not been baptized into this life-giving water and spirit, ask your Chaplain or your ship's visitor how you might be baptized.

3 There was a man named Nicodemus who was a Pharisee and a Jewish leader. ² One night he went to Jesus and said, "Sir, we know that God has sent you to teach us. You could not work these miracles, unless God were with you."

³ Jesus replied, "I tell you for certain that you must be born from above before you can see God's kingdom!"

⁴ Nicodemus asked, "How can a grown man ever be born a second time?"

⁵ Jesus answered:

I tell you for certain that before you can get into God's kingdom, you must be born not only by water, but by the Spirit. ⁶ Humans give life to their children. Yet only God's Spirit can change you into a child of God. ⁷ Don't be surprised when I say that you must be born from above. ⁸ Only God's Spirit gives new life. The Spirit is like the wind that blows wherever it wants to. You can hear the wind, but you don't know where it comes from or where it is going.

⁹ "How can this be?" Nicodemus asked.

¹⁰ Jesus replied:

How can you be a teacher of Israel and not know these things? ¹¹ I tell you for certain that we know what we are talking about because we have seen it ourselves. But none of you will accept what we say. ¹² If you don't believe when I talk to you about things on earth, how can you possibly believe if I talk to you about things in heaven?

¹³ No one has gone up to heaven except the Son of Man, who came down from there. ¹⁴ And the Son of Man must be lifted up, just as

that metal snake was lifted up by Moses in the desert. [15] Then everyone who has faith in the Son of Man will have eternal life.

[16] God loved the people of this world so much that he gave his only Son, so that everyone who has faith in him will have eternal life and never really die. [17] God did not send his Son into the world to condemn its people. He sent him to save them! [18] No one who has faith in God's Son will be condemned. But everyone who doesn't have faith in him has already been condemned for not having faith in God's only Son.

[19] The light has come into the world, and people who do evil things are judged guilty because they love the dark more than the light. [20] People who do evil hate the light and won't come to the light, because it clearly shows what they have done. [21] But everyone who lives by the truth will come to the light, because they want others to know that God is really the one doing what they do.

John 4.3-20
Jesus Provided the Samaritan Woman
With Living Water

True North: You may have many questions for Jesus before you come to believe. This woman did. She wasn't sure that she, as a female and a foreigner, could believe in the same God Jesus did. She learned she could when Jesus said he already knew all about her, and wanted her to believe in him anyway. She received the living water of a new relationship with God. Then she went about telling others, "Come and see Jesus!"

[3] Jesus left Judea and started for Galilee again. [4] This time he had to go through Samaria, [5] and on his way he came to the town of Sychar. It was near the field that Jacob had long ago given to his son Joseph. [6-8] The well that Jacob had dug was still there, and Jesus sat down beside it because he was tired from traveling. It was noon, and after Jesus' disciples had gone into town to buy some food, a Samaritan woman came to draw water from the well.

Jesus asked her, "Would you please give me a drink of water?"

[9] "You are a Jew," she replied, "and I am a Samaritan woman. How can you ask me for a drink of water when Jews and Samaritans won't have anything to do with each other?"

[10] Jesus answered, "You don't know what God wants to give you, and you don't know who is asking you for a drink. If you did, you would ask me for the water that gives life."

[11] "Sir," the woman said, "you don't even have a bucket, and the well is deep. Where are you going to get this life-giving water? [12] Our ancestor Jacob dug this well for us, and his family and animals got water from it. Are you greater than Jacob?"

[13] Jesus answered, "Everyone who drinks this water will get thirsty again. [14] But no one who drinks the water I give will ever be thirsty again. The water I give is like a flowing fountain that gives eternal life."

[15] The woman replied, "Sir, please give me a drink of that water! Then I won't get thirsty and have to come to this well again."

[16] Jesus told her, "Go and bring your husband."

[17-18] The woman answered, "I don't have a husband."

"That's right," Jesus replied, "you're telling the truth. You don't have a husband. You have already been married five times, and the man you are now living with isn't your husband."

[19] The woman said, "Sir, I can see that you are a prophet. [20] My ancestors worshiped on this mountain, but you Jews say Jerusalem is the only place to worship."

[21] Jesus said to her:
Believe me, the time is coming when you won't worship the Father

either on this mountain or in Jerusalem. [22] You Samaritans don't really know the one you worship. But we Jews do know the God we worship, and by using us, God will save the world. [23] But a time is coming, and it is already here! Even now the true worshipers are being led by the Spirit to worship the Father according to the truth. These are the ones the Father is seeking to worship him. [24] God is Spirit, and those who worship God must be led by the Spirit to worship him according to the truth.

[25] The woman said, "I know that the Messiah will come. He is the one we call Christ. When he comes, he will explain everything to us."

[26] "I am that one," Jesus told her, "and I am speaking to you now."

[27] The disciples returned about this time and were surprised to find Jesus talking with a woman. But none of them asked him what he wanted or why he was talking with her.

[28] The woman left her water jar and ran back into town. She said to the people, [29] "Come and see a man who told me everything I have ever done! Could he be the Messiah?" [30] Everyone in town went out to see Jesus.

[31] While this was happening, Jesus' disciples were saying to him, "Teacher, please eat something."

[32] But Jesus told them, "I have food that you don't know anything about."

[33] His disciples started asking each other, "Has someone brought him something to eat?"

[34] Jesus said:

My food is to do what God wants! He is the one who sent me, and I must finish the work that he gave me to do. [35] You may say that there are still four months until harvest time. But I tell you to look, and you will see that the fields are ripe and ready to harvest.

[36] Even now the harvest workers are receiving their reward by gathering a harvest that brings eternal life. Then everyone who planted the seed and everyone who harvests the crop will celebrate together. [37] So the saying proves true, "Some plant the seed, and others harvest the crop." [38] I am sending you to harvest crops in fields where others have done all the hard work.

[39] A lot of Samaritans in that town put their faith in Jesus because the woman had said, "This man told me everything I have ever done." [40] They came and asked him to stay in their town, and he stayed on for two days.

[41] Many more Samaritans put their faith in Jesus because of what they heard him say. [42] They told the woman, "We no longer have faith in Jesus just because of what you told us. We have heard him ourselves, and we are certain that he is the Savior of the world!"

John 7.37-39
Drinking of Jesus' Living Water
Creates a Fountain of Living Water in the Believer

True North: Jesus is living water to quench our spiritual thirst. Knowing Jesus is always having someone there who cares and who can provide when our daily lives make us thirsty for peace, comfort, justice and eternal life. Jesus was referring to this scripture in Isaiah 12.3, "With great joy you people will get water from the wells of victory."

[37] On the last and most important day of the festival, Jesus stood up and shouted, "If you are thirsty, come to me and drink! [38] Have faith in me, and you will have life-giving water flowing from deep inside you, just as the Scriptures say." [39] Jesus was talking about the Holy Spirit, who would be given to everyone that had faith in him. The Spirit had not yet been given to anyone, since Jesus had not yet been given his full glory.

Luke 22.1-23
A Last Meal with the Fruits of Creation

True North: Jesus was willing to die on a cross for us. Before his disciple, Judas, betrayed him. Jesus used wine and bread, the best of God's creation, to show his disciples what he was doing for them in his death. He also promised that he would drink of the fruit of the vine again in God's kingdom. Christians call this meal of Jesus with his disciples, "The Last Supper", or "Holy Communion," or the

"Eucharist" (a Greek word which means thanksgiving). This meal will bless, forgive and free you, for the kingdom has come with Jesus' resurrection. Read the parallels in Matthew 26.1-30; Mark 14.1-26. The story of his arrest, trial, death and resurrection is found in Matthew 26.1-28.20; Mark 14.1-16.8; Luke 19.28-24.53; John 12.1-21.25.

22 The Festival of Thin Bread, also called Passover, was near. [2] The chief priests and the teachers of the Law of Moses were looking for a way to get rid of Jesus, because they were afraid of what the people might do. [3] Then Satan entered the heart of Judas Iscariot, who was one of the twelve apostles.

[4] Judas went to talk with the chief priests and the officers of the temple police about how he could help them arrest Jesus. [5] They were very pleased and offered to pay Judas some money. [6] He agreed and started looking for a good chance to betray Jesus when the crowds were not around.

[7] The day had come for the Festival of Thin Bread, and it was time to kill the Passover lambs. [8] So Jesus said to Peter and John, "Go and prepare the Passover meal for us to eat."

[9] But they asked, "Where do you want us to prepare it?"

[10] Jesus told them, "As you go into the city, you will meet a man carrying a jar of water. Follow him into the house [11] and say to

the owner, 'Our teacher wants to know where he can eat the Passover meal with his disciples.' ¹² The owner will take you upstairs and show you a large room ready for you to use. Prepare the meal there."

¹³ Peter and John left. They found everything just as Jesus had told them, and they prepared the Passover meal.

¹⁴ When the time came for Jesus and the apostles to eat, ¹⁵ he said to them, "I have very much wanted to eat this Passover meal with you before I suffer. ¹⁶ I tell you that I will not eat another Passover meal until it is finally eaten in God's kingdom."

¹⁷ Jesus took a cup of wine in his hands and gave thanks to God. Then he told the apostles, "Take this wine and share it with each other. ¹⁸ I tell you that I will not drink any more wine until God's kingdom comes."

¹⁹ Jesus took some bread in his hands and gave thanks for it. He broke the bread and handed it to his apostles. Then he said, "This is my body, which is given for you. Eat this as a way of remembering me!"

²⁰ After the meal he took another cup of wine in his hands. Then he said, "This is my blood. It is poured out for you, and with it God makes his new agreement. ²¹ The one who will betray me is here at the table with me! ²² The Son of Man will die in the way that has been decided for him, but it will be terrible for the one who betrays him!"

²³ Then the apostles started arguing about who would ever do such a thing.

John 19.28-30
Sour Wine at the Cross

True North: The living water and the wine that Jesus offers us is always good. The wine Jesus was offered when he was dying on the Cross was not good. That sour wine could not save or heal a single person. Jesus drank it to fulfill a prophecy in Psalm 69.21 that the enemies of God's Son would mock him with sour wine. Jesus also drank it to show he had fulfilled the task of saving people that his Father had given him. He drank the cup of suffering right down to the bottom, just as he said he would in John 18.11. Now, he and his Father could offer salvation to all people. Read also the parallels, Matthew 27.45-54; Mark 15.33-39; Luke 23.44-48.

[28] Jesus knew that he had now finished his work. And in order to make the Scriptures come true, he said, "I am thirsty!" [29] A jar of cheap wine was there. Someone then soaked a sponge with the wine and held it up to Jesus' mouth on the stem of a hyssop plant. [30] After Jesus drank the wine, he said, "Everything is done!" He bowed his head and died.

John 19.32-35
Living Water Still Flowed
From Jesus After His Death

True North: Jesus was hung by his arms on a cross to die. He died when he could no longer draw breath. Still his enemies could not stop his death from being a source of life for others. One eyewitness saw that the living water Jesus had talked so much about came out of his side after his death. This person's witness gave hope to everyone. God's love within you is that refreshing, living water Jesus talked about and which poured forth from him even after death. With that living water within you, you will be God's witness to others in this life and your witness will remain after your death. So too, you will be raised to eternal life.

[32] The soldiers first broke the legs of the other two men who were nailed there. [33] But when they came to Jesus, they saw that he was already dead, and they did not break his legs. [34] One of the soldiers

stuck his spear into Jesus' side, and blood and water came out. [35] We know this is true, because it was told by someone who saw it happen. Now you can have faith too.

Luke 24.36-53
Jesus Ate Baked Fish with
His Disciples After the Resurrection

True North: Jesus wants to show his disciples that he was really alive and not an evil spirit or a ghost. What better way to show this than to eat a fish dinner with them!

[36] While Jesus' disciples were talking about what had happened, Jesus appeared and greeted them. [37] They were frightened and terrified because they thought they were seeing a ghost.

[38] But Jesus said, "Why are you so frightened? Why do you doubt? [39] Look at my hands and my feet and see who I am! Touch me and find out for yourselves. Ghosts don't have flesh and bones as you see I have."

[40] After Jesus said this, he showed them his hands and his feet. [41] The disciples were so glad and amazed that they could not believe it. Jesus then asked them, "Do you have something to eat?" [42] They gave him a piece of baked fish. [43] He took it and ate it as they watched.

[44] Jesus said to them, "While I was still with you, I told you that everything written about me in the Law of Moses, the Books of the Prophets, and in the Psalms had to happen."

[45] Then he helped them understand the Scriptures. [46] He told them:
The Scriptures say that the Messiah must suffer, then three days later he will rise from death. [47] They also say that all people of every nation must be told in my name to turn to God, in order to be forgiven. So beginning in Jerusalem, [48] you must tell everything that has happened. [49] I will send you the one my Father has promised, but you must stay in the city until you are given power from heaven.

[50] Jesus led his disciples out to Bethany, where he raised his hands and blessed them. [51] As he was doing this, he left and was taken up to heaven. [52] After his disciples had worshiped him, they returned to Jerusalem and were very happy. [53] They spent their time in the temple, praising God.

SEA READINGS FROM THE NEW TESTAMENT

How Fishers and Seafarers
Witnessed for Jesus

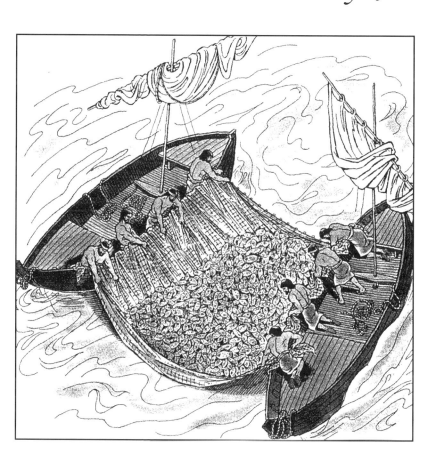

Luke 5.1-11
Jesus Honored the Fishers
He Called as His First Disciples

True North: Jesus honored net fishers by helping them catch fish, which was their calling. Then he taught them about another kind of gathering he wanted them to do. Just as the disciples gathered fish, soon they would be gathering people to become believers. The crowds pressed together to hear Jesus are like fish pressed together in those nets. Jesus can be relied on to gather you in and teach you the good news. Keep an eye out for others who are helping him! Their labor is honorable too! Read also the parallels in Matthew 4.18-22; Mark 1.16-20.

5 Jesus was standing on the shore of Lake Gennesaret, teaching the people as they crowded around him to hear God's message. ² Near the shore he saw two boats left there by some fishermen who had gone to wash their nets. ³ Jesus got into the boat that belonged to Simon and asked him to row it out a little way from the shore. Then Jesus sat down in the boat to teach the crowd.

⁴ When Jesus had finished speaking, he told Simon, "Row the boat out into the deep water and let your nets down to catch some fish."

⁵ "Master," Simon answered, "we have worked hard all night long and have not caught a thing. But if you tell me to, I will let the nets down." ⁶ They did it and caught so many fish that their nets began ripping apart. ⁷ Then they signaled for their partners in the other boat to come and help them. The men came, and together they filled the two boats so full that they both began to sink.

⁸ When Simon Peter saw this happen, he knelt down in front of Jesus and said, "Lord, don't come near me! I am a sinner." ⁹ Peter and everyone with him were completely surprised at all the fish they had caught. ¹⁰ His partners James and John, the sons of Zebedee, were surprised too.

Jesus told Simon, "Don't be afraid! From now on you will bring in people instead of fish." ¹¹ The men pulled their boats up on the shore. Then they left everything and went with Jesus.

SEA READINGS FROM THE NEW TESTAMENT

How Fishers and Seafarers
Witnessed for Jesus

The Apostle Peter

John 21.1-14
The Resurrected Jesus Told His Disciples Where to Fish

True North: *The last thing Jesus did on earth was to help the disciples again find fish. Then Jesus welcomed them to a final meal with him. Are you ready to eat with Jesus?*

21 Jesus later appeared to his disciples along the shore of Lake Tiberias. ² Simon Peter, Thomas the Twin, Nathanael from Cana in Galilee, and the brothers James and John, were there, together with two other disciples. ³ Simon Peter said, "I'm going fishing!"

The others said, "We will go with you." They went out in their boat. But they didn't catch a thing that night.

⁴ Early the next morning Jesus stood on the shore, but the disciples did not realize who he was. ⁵ Jesus shouted, "Friends, have you caught anything?"

"No!" they answered.

⁶ So he told them, "Let your net down on the right side of your boat, and you will catch some fish."

They did, and the net was so full of fish that they could not drag it up into the boat.

⁷ Jesus' favorite disciple told Peter, "It's the Lord!" When Simon heard that it was the Lord, he put on the clothes that he had taken off while he was working. Then he jumped into the water. ⁸ The boat was only about a hundred yards from shore. So the other disciples stayed in the boat and dragged in the net full of fish.

⁹ When the disciples got out of the boat, they saw some bread and a charcoal fire with fish on it. ¹⁰ Jesus told his disciples, "Bring some of the fish you just caught." ¹¹ Simon Peter got back into the boat and dragged the net to shore. In it were one hundred fifty-three large fish, but still the net did not rip.

¹² Jesus said, "Come and eat!" But none of the disciples dared ask who he was. They knew he was the Lord. ¹³ Jesus took the bread in his hands and gave some of it to his disciples. He did the same with the fish. ¹⁴ This was the third time that Jesus appeared to his disciples after he was raised from death.

John 21.15-19
Jesus Netted a Big One—It was Peter!

True North: Jesus was certainly good at spotting fish and disciples. He was also the Good Shepherd. After Jesus and Peter finished their fish breakfast, he challenged and instructed Peter on caring for those who believed in Jesus. Netting fish and gathering sheep are pretty much the same gathering activity. Still, Jesus wanted Peter to gather people for salvation and not so that they might be somebody's breakfast!

¹⁵ When Jesus and his disciples had finished eating, he asked, "Simon son of John, do you love me more than the others do?"

Simon Peter answered, "Yes, Lord, you know I do!"

"Then feed my lambs," Jesus said.

¹⁶ Jesus asked a second time, "Simon son of John, do you love me?"

Peter answered, "Yes, Lord, you know I love you!"

"Then take care of my sheep," Jesus told him.

¹⁷ Jesus asked a third time, "Simon son of John, do you love me?"

Peter was hurt because Jesus had asked him three times if he loved him. So he told Jesus, "Lord, you know everything. You know I love you."

Jesus replied, "Feed my sheep. ¹⁸ I tell you for certain that when you were a young man, you dressed yourself and went wherever you wanted to go. But when you are old, you will hold out your

hands. Then others will wrap your belt around you and lead you where you don't want to go."

¹⁹ Jesus said this to tell how Peter would die and bring honor to God. Then he said to Peter, "Follow me!"

Acts 2.1-6, 36-47
Peter Knew that Water and the Spirit Can Change your Life

True North: When the Holy Spirit fell on the disciples at Pentecost, the Jews in Jerusalem were amazed and curious. Peter told them it meant that God was blessing those who understood that the one who was crucified was the Son of God. Some of the Jews became convinced that they had sinned toward God in Jesus' death. Many repented and were baptized. Give thanks to God, for this same Spirit can fall on you!

2 On the day of Pentecost, all the Lord's followers were together in one place. ² Suddenly there was a noise from heaven like the sound of a mighty wind! It filled the house where they were meeting. ³ Then they saw what looked like fiery tongues moving in all directions, and a tongue came and settled on each person there. ⁴ The Holy Spirit took control of everyone, and they began speaking whatever languages the Spirit let them speak.
⁵ Many religious Jews from every country in the world were living in Jerusalem. ⁶ And when they heard this noise, a crowd gathered. But they were surprised, because they were hearing everything in their own languages.

[Peter said,]
³⁶ Everyone in Israel should then know for certain that God has made Jesus both Lord and Christ, even though you put him to death on a cross.

³⁷ When the people heard this, they were very upset. They asked Peter and the other apostles, "Friends, what shall we do?"

³⁸ Peter said, "Turn back to God! Be baptized in the name of Jesus Christ, so that your sins will be forgiven. Then you will be given the Holy Spirit. ³⁹ This promise is for you and your children. It is for everyone our Lord God will choose, no matter where they live."

[40] Peter told them many other things as well. Then he said, "I beg you to save yourselves from what will happen to all these evil people." [41] On that day about three thousand believed his message and were baptized. [42] They spent their time learning from the apostles, and they were like family to each other. They also broke bread and prayed together.

[43] Everyone was amazed by the many miracles and wonders that the apostles worked. [44] All the Lord's followers often met together, and they shared everything they had. [45] They would sell their property and possessions and give the money to whoever needed it. [46] Day after day they met together in the temple. They broke bread together in different homes and shared their food happily and freely, [47] while praising God. Everyone liked them, and each day the Lord added to their group others who were being saved.

Acts 10.44-48
Can the Holy Spirit Come Upon a Believer Before Water Baptism?

True North: Many Jews who had become Christian first thought that Christian men would still have to be circumcised as the Law required, to show honor and obedience to God. But the Holy Spirit surprised Peter by descending on Gentiles who weren't worshippers of the One God of Israel or followers of the Law. The Spirit fell on both men and women before they were baptized and before the men were circumcised. You can be sure that God loves you and wants you to belong to Christ without your getting circumcised. Instead, there is baptism for everyone. Paul wrote about the difference between circumcision and baptism in Galatians 3.18-29. Read this passage below in the section, "New Testament Guidance for the People of the Sea".

[44] While Peter was still speaking, the Holy Spirit took control of everyone who was listening. [45] Some Jewish followers of the Lord had come with Peter, and they were surprised that the Holy Spirit had been given to Gentiles. [46] Now they were hearing Gentiles speaking unknown languages and praising God.

Peter said, [47] "These Gentiles have been given the Holy Spirit, just as we have! I am certain that no one would dare stop us from baptizing them." [48] Peter ordered them to be baptized in the name of Jesus Christ, and they asked him to stay on for a few days.

SEA READINGS FROM THE NEW TESTAMENT

How Fishers and Seafarers
Witnessed for Jesus

The Apostle Paul

Paul of Tarsus was a highly educated Jewish leader among a group known as the Pharisees. He was also a persecutor of Christians. He believed that, since Jesus died on the Cross as a criminal, he could not be the Son of God. Through Jesus' resurrection he became convinced that he was in error. He was converted and became the seafaring apostle. We have many of his letters to congregations he founded. The Acts of the Apostles describes his missionary journeys to ports in which you may have docked. Here is a list of the places he spoke for God in Christ in 35-60 AD.

Sites of city house churches Paul founded: Philippi, Thessalonia, (in Macedonia) Corinth (in Achaia), Galatia (in Asia Minor). Since we don't have all his letters, we don't know what other congregations he founded in the regions of Achaia, Macedonia, and Asia Minor. He often sent greetings from unspecified house churches to the recipients of his letters. The countries in which these house churches were are now Greece and Turkey.

Sites of house churches we are sure Paul visited from his letters and Acts: Arabia, Damascus in Syria, Antioch in Syria, Caesarea, Tyre, Ptolomais, Jerusalem, Judea, Colossae, Cilicia, Ephesus, Cenchrae (Corinth's seaport), Cyprus, Puteoli (Rome's seaport), Rome. Many of these are seaports.

Towns and islands visited during Paul's missionary journeys starting on the eastern end of the Mediterranean Sea and working west toward Spain: Salamis, Paphos, Perga in Pamphyllia, Attalia, Troas, Assos, Mitylene, Chios, Samos, Trogyllium, Miletus, Cos, Rhodes, Patara, Myra, Sidon, Adramyttium, Cnidus, Salmone, Lasea on Crete, Cauda, Malta, Syracuse on Sicily, Rhegium in Italy.

Paul desired to found a congregation in Spain, but we don't know whether he ever got there. Someone did. Today there are many Christians in Spain.

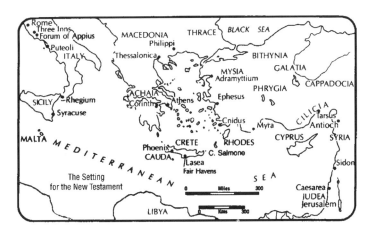

Acts 16.6-15
The Apostle Paul Often Sailed
on the Mediterranean Sea

True North: Paul sailed from Asia Minor (modern Turkey) to the city of Philippi in modern Greece because people needed to hear the Good News there. You will notice in this reading that praying and praising God came first, even for famous apostles.

⁶ Paul and his friends went through Phrygia and Galatia, but the Holy Spirit would not let them preach in Asia. ⁷ After they arrived in Mysia, they tried to go into Bithynia, but the Spirit of Jesus would not let them. ⁸ So they went on through Mysia until they came to Troas.

⁹ During the night, Paul had a vision of someone from Macedonia who was standing there and begging him, "Come over to Macedonia and help us!" ¹⁰ After Paul had seen the vision, we began looking for a way to go to Macedonia. We were sure that God had called us to preach the good news there. ¹¹ We sailed straight from Troas to Samothrace, and the next day we arrived in Neapolis. ¹² From there we went to Philippi, which is a Roman colony in the first district of Macedonia.

We spent several days in Philippi. ¹³ Then on the Sabbath we went outside the city gate to a place by the river, where we thought there would be a Jewish meeting place for prayer. We sat down and talked with the women who came. ¹⁴ One of them was Lydia, who was from the city of Thyatira and sold expensive purple cloth. She was a worshiper of the Lord God, and he made her willing to accept what Paul was saying. ¹⁵ Then after she and her family were baptized, she kept on begging us, "If you think I really do have faith in the Lord, come stay in my home." Finally, we accepted her invitation.

Acts 22.1-21
The Apostle Paul had his
Sins Washed Away When
He Repented and was Baptized

True North: The Apostle Paul was so happy to tell of his conversion that he told the story twice in his own words in the Acts of the Apostles! Both times, Paul spoke of the power of baptism that washed away his sins and of his call by Jesus to be an apostle to the Gentiles. His telling the story twice to different audiences helps you know that it is important to be able to express your faith in different ways in different settings. Read also Acts 9.1-31 and 26.9-11 for the other tellings of his story.

²² "My friends and leaders of our nation, listen as I explain what happened!" ² When the crowd heard Paul speak to them in Aramaic, they became even quieter. Then Paul said:

³ I am a Jew, born and raised in the city of Tarsus in Cilicia. I was a student of Gamaliel and was taught to follow every single law of our ancestors. In fact, I was just as eager to obey God as any of you are today.

⁴ I made trouble for everyone who followed the Lord's Way, and I even had some of them killed. I had others arrested and put in jail. I didn't care if they were men or women. ⁵ The high priest and all the council members can tell you that this is true. They even gave me letters to the Jewish leaders in Damascus, so that I could arrest people there and bring them to Jerusalem to be punished.

⁶ One day about noon I was getting close to Damascus, when a bright light from heaven suddenly flashed around me. ⁷ I fell to the ground and heard a voice asking, "Saul, Saul, why are you so cruel to me?"

⁸ "Who are you?" I answered.

The Lord replied, "I am Jesus from Nazareth! I am the one you are so cruel to." ⁹ The men who were traveling with me saw the light, but did not hear the voice.

¹⁰ I asked, "Lord, what do you want me to do?"

Then he told me, "Get up and go to Damascus. When you get there, you will be told what to do." ¹¹ The light had been so bright that I couldn't see. And the other men had to lead me by the hand to Damascus.

¹² In that city there was a man named Ananias, who faithfully obeyed the Law of Moses and was well liked by all the Jewish people living there. ¹³ He came to me and said, "Saul, my friend, you can now see again!"

At once I could see. ¹⁴ Then Ananias told me, "The God that our ancestors worshiped has chosen you to know what he wants done. He has chosen you to see the One Who Obeys God and to hear his voice. ¹⁵ You must tell everyone what you have seen and heard. ¹⁶ What are you waiting for? Get up! Be baptized, and wash away your sins by praying to the Lord."

¹⁷ After this I returned to Jerusalem and went to the temple to pray. There I had a vision ¹⁸ of the Lord who said to me, "Hurry and leave Jerusalem! The people won't listen to what you say about me."

¹⁹ I replied, "Lord, they know that in many of our meeting places I arrested and beat people who had faith in you. ²⁰ Stephen was killed because he spoke for you, and I stood there and cheered them on. I even guarded the clothes of the men who murdered him."

²¹ But the Lord told me to go, and he promised to send me far away to the Gentiles.

Acts 27.1-28.16
The Apostle Paul was a Chaplain
to Seafarers in a Shipwreck

True North: This very long story is a seafarer's delight. It tells how the Apostle Paul was taken as a prisoner to the emperor in Rome to defend his mission to take Christ to the Gentile nations. In the story are descriptions of sailing itineraries for the Mediterranean Sea, descriptions of ancient grain ships, rigging details, storms, and shipwrecks. There are disputes between the captain and the passengers and the crew. Throughout there is Paul's chaplaincy to seafarers. As you read it, think of the parallels to the great sea stories of Noah and Jonah in the themes of mission and rescue. Then thank God for the courage he gave Paul.

Acts 27.1-12
When Captain Julius took Paul prisoner,
it looked like Paul's fate was no longer in God's hands

27 When it was time for us to sail to Rome, Captain Julius from the Emperor's special troops was put in charge of Paul and the other prisoners. [2] We went aboard a ship from Adramyttium that was about to sail to some ports along the coast of Asia. Aristarchus from Thessalonica in Macedonia sailed on the ship with us.

[3] The next day we came to shore at Sidon. Captain Julius was very kind to Paul. He even let him visit his friends, so they could give him whatever he needed. [4] When we left Sidon, the winds were blowing against us, and we sailed close to the island of Cyprus to be safe from the wind. [5] Then we sailed south of Cilicia and Pamphylia until we came to the port of Myra in Lycia. [6] There the army captain found a ship from Alexandria that was going to Italy. So he ordered us to board that ship.

[7] We sailed along slowly for several days and had a hard time reaching Cnidus. The wind would not let us go any farther in that direction, so we sailed past Cape Salmone, where the island of Crete would protect us from the wind. [8] We went slowly along the coast and finally reached a place called Fair Havens, not far from the town of Lasea.

[9] By now we had already lost a lot of time, and sailing was no longer safe. In fact, even the Great Day of Forgiveness was past. [10] Then Paul spoke to the crew of the ship, "Men, listen to me! If we sail now, our ship and its cargo will be badly damaged, and many lives will be lost." [11] But Julius listened to the captain of the ship and its owner, rather than to Paul.

[12] The harbor at Fair Havens wasn't a good place to spend the winter. Because of this, almost everyone agreed that we should at least try to sail along the coast of Crete as far as Phoenix. It had a harbor that opened toward the southwest and northwest, and we could spend the winter there.

Acts 27.13-26
During a violent storm at sea,
Paul took care of the sailors

[13] When a gentle wind from the south started blowing, the men thought it was a good time to do what they had planned. So they pulled up the anchor, and we sailed along the coast of Crete. [14] But soon a strong wind called "The Northeaster" blew against us from the island. [15] The wind struck the ship, and we could not sail against it. So we let the wind carry the ship.

[16] We went along the island of Cauda on the side that was protected from the wind. We had a hard time holding the lifeboat in place, [17] but finally we got it where it belonged. Then the sailors wrapped ropes around the ship to hold it together. They lowered the sail and let the ship drift along, because they were afraid it might hit the sandbanks in the gulf of Syrtis.

[18] The storm was so fierce that the next day they threw some of the ship's cargo overboard. [19] Then on the third day, with their bare hands they threw overboard some of the ship's gear. [20] For several days we could not see either the sun or the stars. A strong wind kept blowing, and we finally gave up all hope of being saved.

[21] Since none of us had eaten anything for a long time, Paul stood up and told the men:

You should have listened to me! If you had stayed on in Crete, you would not have had this damage and loss. [22] But now I beg you to cheer up, because you will be safe. Only the ship will be lost.

²³ I belong to God, and I worship him. Last night he sent an angel ²⁴ to tell me, "Paul, don't be afraid! You will stand trial before the Emperor. And because of you, God will save the lives of everyone on the ship." ²⁵ Cheer up! I am sure that God will do exactly what he promised. ²⁶ But we will first be shipwrecked on some island.

Acts 27.27-38
After Fourteen Days Without Food in the Storm, Paul still had hope

²⁷ For fourteen days and nights we had been blown around over the Mediterranean Sea. But about midnight the sailors realized that we were getting near land. ²⁸ They measured and found that the water was about one hundred twenty feet deep. A little later they measured again and found it was only about ninety feet. ²⁹ The sailors were afraid that we might hit some rocks, and they let down four anchors

from the back of the ship. Then they prayed for daylight.

³⁰ The sailors wanted to escape from the ship. So they lowered the lifeboat into the water, pretending that they were letting down an anchor from the front of the ship. ³¹ But Paul said to Captain Julius and the soldiers, "If the sailors don't stay on the ship, you won't have any chance to save your lives." ³² The soldiers then cut the ropes that held the lifeboat and let it fall into the sea.

³³ Just before daylight Paul begged the people to eat something. He told them, "For fourteen days you have been so worried that you haven't eaten a thing. ³⁴ I beg you to eat something. Your lives depend on it. Do this and not one of you will be hurt."

[35] After Paul had said this, he took a piece of bread and gave thanks to God. Then in front of everyone, he broke the bread and ate some. [36] They all felt encouraged, and each of them ate something. [37] There were [276] people on the ship, [38] and after everyone had eaten, they threw the cargo of wheat into the sea to make the ship lighter.

Acts 39-44
A shipwreck, but unexpected help

[39] Morning came, and the ship's crew saw a coast that they did not recognize. But they did see a cove with a beach. So they decided to try to run the ship aground on the beach. [40] They cut the anchors loose and let them sink into the sea. At the same time they untied the ropes that were holding the rudders. Next, they raised the sail at the front of the ship and let the wind carry the ship toward the beach. [41] But it ran aground on a sandbank. The front of the ship stuck firmly in the sand, and the rear was being smashed by the force of the waves.

[42] The soldiers decided to kill the prisoners to keep them from swimming away and escaping. [43] But Captain Julius wanted to save Paul's life, and he did not let the soldiers do what they had planned. Instead, he ordered everyone who could swim to dive into the water and head for shore. [44] Then he told the others to hold on to planks of wood or parts of the ship. At last, everyone safely reached shore.

Acts 28.1-9
Dangerous snakes on the Island of Malta,
Just like in the Garden of Eden

28 When we came ashore, we learned that the island was called Malta. [2] The local people were very friendly, and they welcomed us by building a fire, because it was rainy and cold.

[3] After Paul had gathered some wood and had put it on the fire, the heat caused a snake to crawl out, and it bit him on the hand. [4] When the local people saw the snake hanging from Paul's hand, they said to each other, "This man must be a murderer! He didn't drown in the sea, but the goddess of justice will kill him anyway."

[5] Paul shook the snake off into the fire and wasn't harmed. [6] The people kept thinking that Paul would either swell up or suddenly drop

dead. They watched him for a long time, and when nothing happened to him, they changed their minds and said, "This man is a god."

[7] The governor of the island was named Publius, and he owned some of the land around there. Publius was very friendly and welcomed us into his home for three days. [8] His father was in bed, sick with fever and stomach trouble, and Paul went to visit him. Paul healed the man by praying and placing his hands on him.

[9] After this happened, everyone on the island brought their sick people to Paul, and they were all healed. [10] The people were very respectful to us, and when we sailed, they gave us everything we needed.

Acts 28.9-16
Three months to provision, then on to Rome

[11] Three months later we sailed in a ship that had been docked at Malta for the winter. The ship was from Alexandria in Egypt and was known as "The Twin Gods." [12] We arrived in Syracuse and stayed for three days. [13] From there we sailed to Rhegium. The next day a south wind began to blow, and two days later we arrived in Puteoli. [14] There we found some of the Lord's followers, who begged us to stay with them. A week later we left for the city of Rome.

[15] Some of the followers in Rome heard about us and came to meet us at the Market of Appius and at the Three Inns. When Paul saw them, he thanked God and was encouraged.

[16] We arrived in Rome, and Paul was allowed to live in a house by himself with a soldier to guard him.

Romans 8.18-39
Not Even the Deep Seas can
Separate Us from the Love of God

True North: The "powers below" that the Apostle Paul talked about in Romans 8.39 were the seas and all that is frightening below them. Ancient seafarers thought the bottom of the sea was the location of the kingdom of death. Paul knew personally the fear of the sea's power from his own seafaring. But he also knew that God would not abandon those in peril on the sea. We know that too!

[18] I am sure that what we are suffering now cannot compare with the glory that will be shown to us. [19] In fact, all creation is eagerly waiting for God to show who his children are. [20] Meanwhile, creation is confused, but not because it wants to be confused. God made it this way in the hope [21] that creation would be set free from decay and would share in the glorious freedom of his children. [22] We know that all creation is still groaning and is in pain, like a woman about to give birth.

[23] The Spirit makes us sure about what we will be in the future. But now we groan silently, while we wait for God to show that we are his children. This means that our bodies will also be set free. [24] And this hope is what saves us. But if we already have what we hope for, there is no need to keep on hoping. [25] However, we hope for something we have not yet seen, and we patiently wait for it.

[26] In certain ways we are weak, but the Spirit is here to help us. For example, when we don't know what to pray for, the Spirit prays for us in ways that cannot be put into words. [27] All of our thoughts are known to God. He can understand what is in the mind of the Spirit, as the Spirit prays for God's people. [28] We know that God is always at work for the good of everyone who loves him. They are the ones God has chosen for his purpose, [29] and he has always known who his chosen ones would be. He had decided to let them become like his own Son, so that his Son would be the first of many children. [30] God then accepted the people he had already decided to choose, and he has shared his glory with them.

[31] What can we say about all this? If God is on our side, can anyone be against us? [32] God did not keep back his own Son, but he gave him for us. If God did this, won't he freely give us everything else? [33] If God says his chosen ones are acceptable to him, can anyone bring charges against them? [34] Or can anyone condemn them? No indeed! Christ died and was raised to life, and now he is at God's right side, speaking to him for us. [35] Can anything separate us from the love of Christ? Can trouble, suffering, and hard times, or hunger and nakedness, or danger and death? [36] It is exactly as the Scriptures say,

"For you we face death
all day long.

We are like sheep
on their way
to be butchered."

[37] In everything we have won more than a victory because of Christ who loves us. [38] I am sure that nothing can separate us from God's love — not life or death, not angels or spirits, not the present or the future, [39] and not powers above or powers below. Nothing in all creation can separate us from God's love for us in Christ Jesus our Lord!

2 Corinthians 11.25-33
The Apostle Paul Wrote to the Christians
in Corinth About his Seafaring Adventures

True North: Paul's very own letters describe in detail the many dangers from seafaring and from preaching that came from being an apostle to the Gentiles. Paul took on these hardships for the sake of the new life he had found in Christ. He could do this because he knew that he belonged to the Lord in all circumstances.

[25] Three times the Romans beat me with a big stick, and once my enemies stoned me. I have been shipwrecked three times, and I even had to spend a night and a day in the sea. [26] During my many travels, I have been in danger from rivers, robbers, my own people, and foreigners. My life has been in danger in cities, in deserts, at sea, and with people who only pretended to be the Lord's followers. [27] I have worked and struggled and spent many sleepless nights. I have gone hungry and thirsty and often had nothing to eat. I have been cold from not having enough clothes to keep me warm. [28] Besides everything else, each day I am burdened down, worrying about all the churches. [29] When others are weak, I am weak too. When others are tricked into sin, I get angry. [30] If I have to brag, I will brag about how weak I am. [31] God, the Father of our Lord Jesus, knows I am not lying. And God is to be praised forever! [32] The governor of Damascus at the time of King Aretas had the city gates guarded, so that he could capture me. [33] But I escaped by being let down in a basket through a window in the city wall.

SEA READINGS FROM THE NEW TESTAMENT

New Testament Guidance
for the People of the Sea

Matthew 5.43-48
Act Like your Father in Heaven

True North: How do you pray for enemies? You pray that they might be protected, comforted and empowered for godliness. You pray that your Father in heaven might bless them to know, desire and live out divine fairness. You pray that they too might be forgiven and raised from death to new life. You pray that you might be forgiven your sins also. See also the parallel, Luke 6.27-36.

43 You have heard people say, "Love your neighbors and hate your enemies." 44 But I tell you to love your enemies and pray for anyone who mistreats you. 45 Then you will be acting like your Father in heaven. He makes the sun rise on both good and bad people. And he sends rain for the ones who do right and for the ones who do wrong. 46 If you love only those people who love you, will God reward you for that? Even tax collectors love their friends. 47 If you greet only your friends, what's so great about that? Don't even unbelievers do that? 48 But you must always act like your Father in heaven.

Matthew 7.24-29
A House by the Sea of Life?
Be Careful what you Build on!

True North: If you build a house of faith on the rock of Jesus' words and do what he asks of you, you won't be flooded out even when the greatest waves of worldly care and oppression lap around you.

24 Anyone who hears and obeys these teachings of mine is like a wise person who built a house on solid rock. 25 Rain poured down, rivers flooded, and winds beat against that house. But it did not fall, because it was built on solid rock.

26 Anyone who hears my teachings and doesn't obey them is like a foolish person who built a house on sand. 27 The rain poured

down, the rivers flooded, and the winds blew and beat against that house. Finally, it fell with a crash.

²⁸ When Jesus finished speaking, the crowds were surprised at his teaching. ²⁹ He taught them like someone with authority, and not like their teachers of the Law of Moses.

Matthew 28.16-20
The Great Commission:
Your Sailing Papers from Jesus

True North: Why would believers do what Jesus asks of us and go where Jesus asks us to go? This passage says it is because he has all authority on earth and in heaven. Why was baptizing in water with God's Holy Spirit the sign Jesus chose to mark us as Christians? It is because without God's help through Christ, we cannot make water obey our will. We cannot control the sea. We cannot endure a flood like Noah did and save ourselves. We cannot be swallowed by a great fish like Jonah and rise again. We cannot walk on water. We cannot change water into wine. So, God has given us baptism so that where we might have sailed into trouble, there is rescue. Where we might have not gotten all the dirt or sin off us, there is now cleanliness and purity. Where we might have drowned, there is resurrection. Where we might not have been wanted by anyone, now we have our sailing papers from Jesus. Baptism puts into water words all God has done for us and marks it with the power of Christ and the Holy Spirit. We cannot do any of this for ourselves!

¹⁶ Jesus' eleven disciples went to a mountain in Galilee, where Jesus had told them to meet him. ¹⁷ They saw him and worshiped him, but some of them doubted.

¹⁸ Jesus came to them and said:

I have been given all authority in heaven and on earth! ¹⁹ Go to the people of all nations and make them my disciples. Baptize them in the name of the Father, the Son, and the Holy Spirit, ²⁰ and teach them to do everything I have told you. I will be with you always, even until the end of the world.

Mark 7.14-23
Watch Your Mouth!

True North: Jesus put an end to the food laws of Leviticus 11.9-19 that said you couldn't eat shellfish. He saw a different problem and a different solution. Do you agree with Jesus?

[14] Jesus called the crowd together again and said, "Pay attention and try to understand what I mean. [15-16] The food that you put into your mouth doesn't make you unclean and unfit to worship God. The bad words that come out of your mouth are what make you unclean."

[17] After Jesus and his disciples had left the crowd and had gone into the house, they asked him what these sayings meant. [18] He answered, "Don't you know what I am talking about by now? You surely know that the food you put into your mouth cannot make you unclean. [19] It doesn't go into your heart, but into your stomach, and then out of your body." By saying this, Jesus meant that all foods were fit to eat.

[20] Then Jesus said:

What comes from your heart is what makes you unclean. [21] Out of your heart come evil thoughts, vulgar deeds, stealing, murder, [22] unfaithfulness in marriage, greed, meanness, deceit, indecency, envy, insults, pride, and foolishness. [23] All of these come from your heart, and they are what make you unfit to worship God.

Luke 11.9-13
Jesus Taught,
"God's Gifts are Better than the Best Fish!"

True North: To pray is to knock on heaven's door knowing the door is already open. Read also Matthew 7.7-11.

[9] So I tell you to ask and you will receive, search and you will find, knock and the door will be opened for you. [10] Everyone who asks will receive, everyone who searches will find, and the door will be opened for everyone who knocks. [11] Which one of you fathers would give your hungry child a snake if the child asked for a fish? [12] Which one of you

would give your child a scorpion if the child asked for an egg? [13] As bad as you are, you still know how to give good gifts to your children. But your heavenly Father is even more ready to give the Holy Spirit to anyone who asks.

Luke 17.1-6
It is Better to have Faith Enough to Plant a Tree in the Sea Than to be Thrown into that Sea for Sinning

True North: Your choice: Having faith can grow trees in the sea. Doing evil will lead you to a watery grave.

17 Jesus said to his disciples:

There will always be something that causes people to sin. But anyone who causes them to sin is in for trouble. A person who causes even one of my little followers to sin [2] would be better off thrown into the ocean with a heavy stone tied around their neck. [3] So be careful what you do.

Correct any followers of mine who sin, and forgive the ones who say they are sorry. [4] Even if one of them mistreats you seven times in one day and says, "I am sorry," you should still forgive that person.

[5] The apostles said to the Lord, "Make our faith stronger!"

[6] Jesus replied:

If you had faith no bigger than a tiny mustard seed, you could tell this mulberry tree to pull itself up, roots and all, and to plant itself in the ocean. And it would!

Romans 6.1-12
No Longer Sinking Down

True North: Baptism into Christ gains us eternal life. You will be free from Sin's boss, Captain Death, who now makes your life a repeating shipwreck. This text is the background for the famous hymn, "Amazing Grace", written by Captain John Newton, 1725-1801. This hymn is about his rescue from sin by the grace of God. Later, God helped him realize that his faith in Jesus meant he could no longer be captain of ships that carried captured Africans to make them slaves. He learned that slavery was inhuman treatment of the very people that God had created and loved.

[6] What should we say? Should we keep on sinning, so that God's wonderful kindness will show up even better? [2] No, we should not! If we are dead to sin, how can we go on sinning? [3] Don't you know that all who share in Christ Jesus by being baptized also share in his death? [4] When we were baptized, we died and were buried with Christ. We were baptized, so that we would live a new life, as Christ was raised to life by the glory of God the Father.

[5] If we shared in Jesus' death by being baptized, we will be raised to life with him. [6] We know that the persons we used to be were nailed to the cross with Jesus. This was done, so that our sinful bodies would no longer be the slaves of sin. [7] We know that sin doesn't have power over dead people.

[8] As surely as we died with Christ, we believe we will also live with him. [9] We know that death no longer has any power over Christ. He died and was raised to life, never again to die. [10] When Christ died, he died for sin once and for all. But now he is alive, and

he lives only for God. [11] In the same way, you must think of yourselves as dead to the power of sin. But Christ Jesus has given life to you, and you live for God.

[12] Don't let sin rule your body. After all, your body is bound to die, so don't obey its desires

I Corinthians 10.1-11
Once You've Walked Through
God's Cleansing Waters, Will you Ever Sin Again?

True North: Paul told a Bible story of how God's people were rescued from Egypt, but then fell into idolatry by eating at a feast they prepared for an idol. They thought Red Sea baptism meant they could do anything they wanted and God wouldn't object. Paul reminded the Christians in Corinth how quickly believers could go from salvation to sin. So, what is the solution? It is to join in the Lord's Supper. There you will have a blessed meal with Christ, a foretaste of the feast to come with God, refreshment for your days and forgiveness for your continuing sin.

Remember, too, that every one who is at the Lord's Supper is especially invited by Jesus, including you! So be sure to treat everyone there as an honored guest for you are all equal in Jesus' eyes. "All of us have sinned and fallen short of God's glory. But God treats us much better than we deserve and because of Christ Jesus he freely accepts us and sets us free from our sins" (Rm 3.23-24). You may read the whole story of Israel's idolatry in the wilderness in Exodus 32.1-35.

[10] Friends, I want to remind you that all of our ancestors walked under the cloud and went through the sea. [2] This was like being baptized and becoming followers of Moses. [3] All of them also ate the same spiritual food [4] and drank the same spiritual drink, which flowed from the spiritual rock that followed them. That rock was Christ. [5] But most of them did not please God. So they died, and their bodies were scattered all over the desert.

[6] What happened to them is a warning to keep us from wanting to do the same evil things. [7] They worshiped idols, just as the Scriptures say, "The people sat down to eat and drink. Then they got up to dance around." So don't worship idols. [8] Some of those people did shameful things, and in a single day about twenty-three thousand of them died. Don't do shameful things as they did. [9] And don't try to test Christ, as

some of them did and were later bitten by poisonous snakes. [10] Don't even grumble, as some of them did and were killed by the destroying angel. [11] These things happened to them as a warning to us. All this was written in the Scriptures to teach us who live in these last days.

Galatians 3.26-29
All You who are Baptized
are Equal to One Another

True North: While at work aboard ship, an able-bodied seafarer, a chief mate and a captain may not consider each other family members because their status is different. In Christ's world, you are all one body, dressed by Christ with everyone wearing the same uniform: Christ.

[26] All of you are God's children because of your faith in Christ Jesus. [27] And when you were baptized, it was as though you had put on Christ in the same way you put on new clothes. [28] Faith in Christ Jesus is what makes each of you equal with each other, whether you are a Jew or a Greek, a slave or a free person, a man or a woman. [29] So if you belong to Christ, you are now part of Abraham's family, and you will be given what God has promised.

Titus 3.3-7
God Saved us Through the
Waters of Rebirth and Renewal

True North: From hating ourselves to being loved by God. What a sea change!

3 Remind your people to obey the rulers and authorities and not to be rebellious. They must always be ready to do something helpful [2] and not say cruel things or argue. They should be gentle and kind to everyone. [3] We used to be stupid, disobedient, and foolish, as well as slaves of all sorts of desires and pleasures. We were evil and jealous. Everyone hated us, and we hated everyone.

[4]   God our Savior showed us
          how good and kind he is.

5 He saved us because
       of his mercy,
   and not because
   of any good things
       that we have done.

   God washed us by the power
       of the Holy Spirit.
   He gave us new birth
       and a fresh beginning.
6 God sent Jesus Christ
   our Savior
       to give us his Spirit.

7 Jesus treated us much better
       than we deserve.
   He made us acceptable to God
   and gave us the hope
       of eternal life.

1 Peter 3.15-22
Baptism is Like Noah's Flood.
It Washes us Clean

True North: *When Christ's body was under death's power, his spirit was busy preaching Good News to the dead. You are not that far away from God! Prepare for this hope in your life!*

[15] Honor Christ and let him be the Lord of your life.

Always be ready to give an answer when someone asks you about your hope. [16] Give a kind and respectful answer and keep your conscience clear. This way you will make people ashamed for saying bad things about your good conduct as a follower of Christ. [17] You are better off to obey God and suffer for doing right than to suffer for doing wrong.

[18]   Christ died once for our sins.
An innocent person died
        for those who are guilty.
Christ did this
        to bring you to God,
when his body
        was put to death
and his spirit
        was made alive.

[19] Christ then preached to the spirits that were being kept in prison. [20] They had disobeyed God while Noah was building the boat, but God had been patient with them. Eight people went into that boat and were brought safely through the flood.

[21] Those flood waters were like baptism that now saves you. But baptism is more than just washing your body. It means turning to God with a clear conscience, because Jesus Christ was raised from death. [22] Christ is now in heaven, where he sits at the right side of God. All angels, authorities, and powers are under his control.

Hebrews 11.1-16, 23-29, 39
Both Noah the Seafarer and
Moses who Parted the Red Sea
Had Faith and Pleased God

True North: Here is a brief history of God and some of God's most faithful followers. Early Christians honored Noah and Moses as models for their own faith. They were convinced by Jesus' death and resurrection that they could also be faithful to God. These promises are sure for you too. In the breaks in the text are more faith stories for you to discover.

11 Faith makes us sure of what we hope for and gives us proof of what we cannot see. [2] It was their faith that made our ancestors pleasing to God.

[3] Because of our faith, we know that the world was made at God's command. We also know that what can be seen was made out of what cannot be seen.

[4] Because Abel had faith, he offered God a better sacrifice than Cain did. God was pleased with him and his gift, and even though Abel is now dead, his faith still speaks for him.

[5] Enoch had faith and did not die. He pleased God, and God took him up to heaven. That's why his body was never found. [6] But without faith no one can please God. We must believe that God is real and that he rewards everyone who searches for him.

[7] Because Noah had faith, he was warned about something that had not yet happened. He obeyed and built a boat that saved him and his family. In this way the people of the world were judged, and Noah was given the blessings that come to everyone who pleases God.

[8] Abraham had faith and obeyed God. He was told to go to the land that God had said would be his, and he left for a country he had never seen. [9] Because Abraham had faith, he lived as a stranger in the promised land. He lived there in a tent, and so did Isaac and Jacob, who were later given the same promise. [10] Abraham did this, because he was waiting for the eternal city that God had planned and built.

[11] Even when Sarah was too old to have children, she had faith that God would do what he had promised, and she had a son. [12] Her

husband Abraham was almost dead, but he became the ancestor of many people. In fact, there are as many of them as there are stars in the sky or grains of sand along the beach.

[13] Every one of those people died. But they still had faith, even though they had not received what they had been promised. They were glad just to see these things from far away, and they agreed that they were only strangers and foreigners on this earth. [14] When people talk this way, it is clear that they are looking for a place to call their own. [15] If they had been talking about the land where they had once lived, they could have gone back at any time. [16] But they were looking forward to a better home in heaven. That's why God wasn't ashamed for them to call him their God. He even built a city for them.

[23] Because Moses' parents had faith, they kept him hidden until he was three months old. They saw that he was a beautiful child, and they were not afraid to disobey the king's orders. [24] Then after Moses grew up, his faith made him refuse to be called Pharaoh's grandson. [25] He chose to be mistreated with God's people instead of having the good time that sin could bring for a little while. [26] Moses knew that the treasures of Egypt were not as wonderful as what he would receive from suffering for the Messiah, and he looked forward to his reward. [27] Because of his faith, Moses left Egypt. Moses had seen the invisible God and wasn't afraid of the king's anger. [28] His faith also made him celebrate Passover. He sprinkled the blood of animals on the doorposts, so that the first-born sons of the people of Israel would not be killed by the destroying angel.

[29] Because of their faith, the people walked through the Red Sea on dry land. But when the Egyptians tried to do it, they were drowned.

[39] All of them pleased God because of their faith! But still they died without being given what had been promised. [40] This was because God had something better in store for us. And he did not want them to reach the goal of their faith without us.

James 3.1-12
Strive to Control your Tongue
Like a Captain Controls a Ship

True North: Imagine your tongue as a rudder that steers you. Are you pleased with its "true north"?

3 My friends, we should not all try to become teachers. In fact, teachers will be judged more strictly than others. ² All of us do many wrong things. But if you can control your tongue, you are mature and able to control your whole body.

³ By putting a bit into the mouth of a horse, we can turn the horse in different directions. ⁴ It takes strong winds to move a large sailing ship, but the captain uses only a small rudder to make it go in any direction. ⁵ Our tongues are small too, and yet they brag about big things.

It takes only a spark to start a forest fire! ⁶ The tongue is like a spark. It is an evil power that dirties the rest of the body and sets a person's entire life on fire with flames that come from hell itself. ⁷ All kinds of animals, birds, reptiles, and sea creatures can be tamed and have been tamed. ⁸ But our tongues get out of control. They are restless and evil, and always spreading deadly poison.

⁹⁻¹⁰ My dear friends, with our tongues we speak both praises and curses. We praise our Lord and Father, and we curse people who were created to be like God, and this isn't right. ¹¹ Can clean water and dirty water both flow from the same spring? ¹² Can a fig tree produce olives or a grapevine produce figs? Does fresh water come from a well full of salt water?

James 1.5-8; 5.7-20
Trust in God Smooths a Seafarer's Tempestuous Life

True North: While you wait on the Lord to come again (5.7), you can be part of a community of believers aboard ship. Plan times to praise God and to pray for one another with confidence. Let God guide your faith so it may be like a peaceful swell and not like a storm-tossed ocean wave. Confess to one another, and pray for one another. Your prayers are powerful for others. You will be able, with prayer, by the help of God, to lead your companions back to safe harbor in Christ.

James 1.5-8

⁵ If any of you need wisdom, you should ask God, and it will be given to you. God is generous and won't correct you for asking. ⁶ But when you ask for something, you must have faith and not doubt. Anyone who doubts is like an ocean wave tossed around in a storm. ⁷⁻⁸ If you are that kind of person, you can't make up your mind, and you surely can't be trusted. So don't expect the Lord to give you anything at all.

James 5.7-20

⁷ My friends, be patient until the Lord returns. Think of farmers who wait patiently for the spring and summer rains to make their valuable crops grow. ⁸ Be patient like those farmers and don't give up. The Lord will soon be here! ⁹ Don't grumble about each other or you will be judged, and the judge is right outside the door.

¹⁰ My friends, follow the example of the prophets who spoke for the Lord. They were patient, even when they had to suffer. ¹¹ In fact, we praise the ones who endured the most. You remember how

patient Job was and how the Lord finally helped him. The Lord did this because he is so merciful and kind.

¹² My friends, above all else, don't take an oath. You must not swear by heaven or by earth or by anything else. "Yes" or "No" is all you need to say. If you say anything more, you will be condemned.

¹³ If you are having trouble, you should pray. And if you are feeling good, you should sing praises. ¹⁴ If you are sick, ask the church leaders to come and pray for you. Ask them to put olive oil on you in the name of the Lord. ¹⁵ If you have faith when you pray for sick people, they will get well. The Lord will heal them, and if they have sinned, he will forgive them.

¹⁶ If you have sinned, you should tell each other what you have done. Then you can pray for one another and be healed. The prayer of an innocent person is powerful, and it can help a lot. ¹⁷ Elijah was just as human as we are, and for three and a half years his prayers kept the rain from falling. ¹⁸ But when he did pray for rain, it fell from the skies and made the crops grow.

¹⁹ My friends, if any followers have wandered away from the truth, you should try to lead them back. ²⁰ If you turn sinners from the wrong way, you will save them from death, and many of their sins will be forgiven.

SEA READINGS ABOUT
GOD'S ETERNAL REIGN

In the biblical texts you've read so far, there have been many descriptions of the powerful sea and the blessings of fresh water. Seafarers and fishers have also always hoped that one sign of God's eternal kindness would be the sea becoming finally and totally peaceful. For the sea was threatening to seafarers and fishers every day while empires rose and fell only occasionally. You will find below that the prophets who talked about the coming of God's eternal reign combined the descriptions of the powerful sea and the blessings of fresh water with the images of empires as evil port cities and mighty sea monsters. As you will read below, not all these prophets had the same vision about what will happen to this world when God's eternal reign ends all evil.

SEA READINGS ABOUT GOD'S ETERNAL REIGN

How the Prophets Isaiah and Ezekiel Proclaimed God's Eternal Reign

When Christians think about the end of time, they often have these two questions. Will the world ever fully know God's kindness? Will there be a physical end to this earth? The Major Prophets, Isaiah, Jeremiah and Ezekiel said, "Yes" to the first question. God's great kindness would come about in this world. The prophets were sure that God would help believers to bring about peace. The believers could not do this without God's help. God would act to destroy all greedy empires. The Major Prophets said, "No" to the second question about the physical end of the earth. They did not prophesy that the earth would end before God got it all sorted out. There would be a peaceable kingdom on this earth. Believers would live obediently before God and would have many children. These prophets did not believe that the earth would be destroyed or that they would be raised from the dead to a heavenly realm.

Isaiah 21.1-15
Babylon is Fallen!

True North: In the 8th century before Christ, the prophet Isaiah saw in a vision the fall of mighty Babylon, the city and empire which held Israel captive. Isaiah prophesied about three events he saw in this vision. First, Babylon, an evil city in the desert beside the sea (the Persian Gulf), would be overthrown by God's action. Second, the conquerors would be acting on God's orders, even though they did not believe in the one God. Three, God would direct the desert dwelling Arabs to bring the gift of fresh water from the desert to the thirsty former captives. Isaiah was confident that all three of these things would come to pass to create a more peaceful earth. See also Isaiah 41.1-7.

21 This is a message about
   a desert beside the sea:

   Enemies from a hostile nation
   attack like a whirlwind
     from the Southern Desert.
2 What a horrible vision
     was shown to me —
   a vision of betrayal
     and destruction.
   Tell Elam and Media
   to surround and attack
     the Babylonians.
   The Lord has sworn to end
     the suffering they caused.

3 I'm in terrible pain
     like a woman giving birth.
   I'm shocked and hurt so much
     that I can't hear or see.
4 My head spins; I'm horrified!
   Early evening, my favorite time,
     has become a nightmare.

5 In Babylon the high officials

were having a feast.
They were eating and drinking,
    when someone shouted,
"Officers, take your places!
    Grab your shields."

6   The Lord said to me,
"Send guards to find out
    what's going on.
7   When they see cavalry troops
    and columns of soldiers
on donkeys and camels,
    tell them to be ready!"

8   Then a guard said,
"I have stood day and night
    on this watchtower, Lord.
9   Now I see column after column
    of cavalry troops."

Right away someone shouted,
    "Babylon has fallen!
Every idol in the city
    lies broken on the ground."

10   Then I said, "My people,
    you have suffered terribly,
but I have a message for you
from the Lord All-Powerful,
    the God of Israel."

13 This is a message for Arabs
who live in the barren desert
    in the region of Dedan:
You must order your caravans
14 to bring water for those
who are thirsty.
You people of Tema

Must bring food
For the hungry refugees.
¹⁵ They are worn out and weary
from being chased by enemies
with swords and arrows.

Isaiah 23.1-18
You Seafarers will have to Become Farmers!

True North: What a threat to the income of seafarers! Tyre, a port city, would be destroyed because it drew honor to itself rather than offering honor to God. Isaiah's message about Tyre pointed out that God was watching to see that people were humble and just. Is the warning to Tyre something seafarers now need to think about even now? Yes. God is asking us to be active guardians for peace and justice for a better world for everyone everywhere. It may feel much safer to do what a shipmate, a captain or a shipping company might ask you to do, even if it is not a humble or a just thing to do. But God wants us to be humble and just while working with shipmates, while following regulations and while on shore leave. Otherwise, we allow port cities like Tyre to grow in wickedness and to prostitute themselves when we turn away from justice.

23   This is a message
from distant islands
      about the city of Tyre:
Cry, you seagoing ships!
Tyre and its houses
      lie in ruins.
²   Mourn in silence,
you shop owners of Sidon,
      you people on the coast.
Your sailors crossed oceans,
      making your city rich.
³   Your merchants sailed the seas,
making you wealthy by trading
      with nation after nation.
They brought back grain
      that grew along the Nile.

4   Sidon, you are a mighty fortress
                built along the sea.
        But you will be disgraced
        like a married woman
                who never had children.

5   When Egypt hears about Tyre,
                it will tremble.
6   All of you along the coast
        had better cry and sail
                far across the ocean.
7   Can this be the happy city
                that has stood for centuries?
        Its people have spread
                to distant lands;
8   its merchants were kings
                honored all over the world.
        Who planned to destroy Tyre?
9   The Lord All-Powerful planned it
                to bring shame and disgrace
        to those who are honored
                by everyone on earth.
10   People of Tyre,
                your harbor is destroyed!
        You will have to become farmers
        just like the Egyptians.
11   The Lord's hand has reached
        across the sea,
                upsetting the nations.
        He has given a command
        to destroy fortresses
                in the land of Canaan.
12   The Lord has said
                to the people of Sidon,
        "Your celebrating is over —
                you are crushed.
        Even if you escape to Cyprus,
                you won't find peace."

¹³ Look what the Assyrians have done to Babylonia! They have attacked, destroying every palace in the land. Now wild animals live among the ruins. ¹⁴ Not a fortress will be left standing, so tell all the seagoing ships to mourn.

¹⁵ The city of Tyre will be forgotten for seventy years, which is the lifetime of a king. Then Tyre will be like that evil woman in the song:

¹⁶   You're gone and forgotten,
               you evil woman!
     So strut through the town,
               singing and playing
     your favorite tune
               to be remembered again.

¹⁷ At the end of those seventy years, the Lord will let Tyre get back into business. The city will be like a woman who sells her body to everyone of every nation on earth, ¹⁸ but none of what is earned will be kept in the city. That money will belong to the Lord, and it will be used to buy more than enough food and good clothes for those who worship the Lord.

Isaiah 26.19-27.1
A Sea Monster With a Double Face

True North: *Since the creation, Leviathan symbolized the chaos that was there before God acted to separate and calm the waters. Isaiah saw that at time's end Leviathan would not be a playful fish under God's command. The sea monster would try to rule the waters again. Then God would give life to those caught in death's kingdom under the sea by slaying this chaos monster. God can slay the chaos in your life too.*

Isaiah prophesied to Israel:
¹⁹   Your people will rise to life!
     Tell them to leave their graves
               and celebrate with shouts.
     You refresh the earth
     like morning dew;
               you give life to the dead.

20   Go inside and lock the doors,
        my people.
    Hide there for a little while,
    until the Lord
        is no longer angry.

21   The Lord will come out
    to punish everyone on earth
        for their sins.
    And when he does,
    those who did violent crimes
        will be known and punished.

27   On that day, Leviathan,
        the sea monster,
    will squirm and try to escape,
    but the Lord will kill him
        with a cruel, sharp sword.

Isaiah 55.1-13
Come and Drink the Water!

True North: *What will it be like when all enemies are conquered and God's peaceful reign begins on this earth? Isaiah prophesied that it would be like having unexpected fresh water in the desert. God's water words would refresh the earth. You, too will be refreshed when you read your Bible as words from One who loves and protects you. See also Isaiah 41.8-20.*

1   If you are thirsty,
        Come and drink the water!
    If you don't have any money,
        Come, eat what you want!
    Drink wine and milk
        Without paying a cent.

2   Why waste your money
        on what really isn't food?
    Why work hard for something
        that doesn't satisfy?

Listen carefully to me
And you will enjoy
    The very best foods.

3   Pay close attention!
        Come to me and live.
I will promise you
The eternal love and loyalty
        That I promised David.

4   I made him the leader and ruler
of the nations;
        he was my witness to them.

5   You will call out to the nations
you have never known.
And they have never known you.
But they will come running
        Because I am the Lord,
The holy God of Israel,
        And I have honored you.

6   Turn to the Lord!
He can still be found!
        Call out to God! He is near.

7   Give up your crooked ways
        and your evil thoughts.
Return to the Lord our God.
He will be merciful
        And forgive your sins.

8   The Lord says:
"My thoughts and my ways
        Are not like yours.

9   Just as the heavens
        are higher than the earth,
my thoughts and my ways,
        are higher than yours.

10   "Rain and snow fall from the sky.
But they don't return
        Without watering the earth
that produces seed to plant

and grain to eat.

11   That's how it is with my words.
>> They don't return to me
without doing everything
>> I sent them to do.
12   When you are set free,
you will celebrate
>> and travel home in peace.
Mountains and hills will sing
as you pass by,
>> and trees will clap.
13   Cypress and myrtle trees
will grow in the fields
>> once covered by thorns.
And then those trees will stand
As a lasting witness
>> To the glory of the Lord.

Ezekiel 47.1-12
Can Salt Water Become Fresh Water?
With God's Help!

True North: Ezekiel's vision is amazing. God's action to save doesn't simply dilute the sins or the evil that you have done or that has been done to you. It will change you entirely so you feel fresh and sweet. From salt to fresh! From sweat to sweet! So, drink regularly from the freshness of God!

47 The man took me back to the temple, where I saw a stream flowing from under the entrance. It began in the south part of the temple, where it ran past the altar and continued east through the courtyard.

² We walked out of the temple area through the north gate and went around to the east gate. I saw the small stream of water flowing east from the south side of the gate.

³ The man walked east, then took out his measuring stick and measured five hundred sixty yards downstream. He told me to wade through the stream there, and the water came up to my ankles. ⁴ Then he measured another five hundred sixty yards downstream, and told

me to wade through it there. The water came up to my knees. Another five hundred sixty yards downstream the water came up to my waist. ⁵ Another five hundred sixty yards downstream, the stream had become a river that could be crossed only by swimming. ⁶ The man said, "Ezekiel, son of man, pay attention to what you've seen."

We walked to the riverbank, ⁷ where I saw dozens of trees on each side. ⁸ The man said:

This water flows eastward to the Jordan River valley and empties into the Dead Sea, where it turns the salt water into fresh water. ⁹ Wherever this water flows, there will be all kinds of animals and fish, because it will bring life and fresh water to the Dead Sea. ¹⁰ From En-Gedi to Eneglaim, people will fish in the sea and dry their nets along the coast. There will be as many kinds of fish in the Dead Sea as there are in the Mediterranean Sea. ¹¹ But the marshes along the shore will remain salty, so that people can use the salt from them.

¹² Fruit trees will grow all along this river and produce fresh fruit every month. The leaves will never dry out, because they will always have water from the stream that flows from the temple, and they will be used for healing people.

SEA READINGS ABOUT
GOD'S ETERNAL REIGN

How the Prophet Daniel Interpreted Dreams of God's Eternal Reign

In Daniel's time, the holy people were a conquered nation. They were captive to other powers. They did not have a kingdom of their own. Still, God rescued faithful individuals like Daniel from the lion's den (Dn 6.1-28). God gave Daniel the ability to interpret the dreams of Gentile kings, like Nebuchadnezzar, so that they would know what God thought of their kingdoms (Dn 2.1-5.31). Daniel also had visions of his own and visitations from God's warrior angels. One angel showed Daniel that each nation had its own warrior angel to guard it. Heavenly warfare took place between these angels (10.1-20). These angels signified that earthly warfare affected the heavens and heavenly warfare affected the earth, so that evil could only be resolved by the Supreme Ruler, God. Through these dreams and visions, Daniel was given an understanding of God's eternal reign that was different from that of the prophets Isaiah, Jeremiah and Ezekiel. Daniel would have said "No" to the first question about how God would intercede at the end of time. He did not see that God's kindness would ever be fully here on this earth. Daniel would have said, "Yes" to the second question about the physical end of the earth. He was told in his vision that the earth he knew would be completely destroyed. Despite this sad and terrifying understanding of the end of the earth, Daniel had confidence that God would raise believers from death. You've probably felt at times like Daniel, trapped by authorities and foreign nations. But you have the same resources Daniel did. By praying and staying in touch with other Christians, you will keep in contact with the One who untangles the daily traps that ensnare you, who ends all evil and will raise you to new life.

Daniel 7.1-14
Worldy Chaos Comes from Watery Chaos;
Final Order Will Come from Heaven

True North: Daniel had a vision of beasts rising from the sea. They represented evil power and chaos. Daniel did not understand the origin or desires of these giant beasts. Why would they arise from the kingdom of the dead to terrify and control God's people? The prophet Daniel saw that the Eternal God would destroy these powers from the sea. At the end of time God would welcome one in the form of a Son of Man (a human being) who would come with the clouds from on high and who would be given all power, glory and honor by God. He would rule without end from the heavens. Daniel did not think this would happen until long after he was dead. We worry about such beasts today. Think of the movies you have seen about monsters from the deep. When you look over the side of the ship and worry what is in depths of the ocean where you cannot see, you are having a feeling similar to Daniel's. John of Patmos saw these same beasts rising from the sea in his vision of the end of time, and also saw God conquering them and making the oceans safe. Read Revelation 13.1-18.

7 ¹-² Daniel wrote:

In the first year of King Belshazzar of Babylonia, I had some dreams and visions while I was asleep one night, and I wrote them down.

The four winds were stirring up the mighty sea, ³ when suddenly four powerful beasts came out of the sea. Each beast was different. ⁴ The first was like a lion with the wings of an eagle. As I watched, its wings were pulled off. Then it was lifted to an upright position and made to stand on two feet, just like a human, and it was given a human mind.

⁵ The second beast looked like a bear standing on its hind legs. It held three ribs in its teeth, and it was told, "Attack! Eat all the flesh you want."

⁶ The third beast was like a leopard — except that it had four wings and four heads. It was given authority to rule.

⁷ The fourth beast was stronger and more terrifying than the others. Its huge teeth were made of iron, and what it didn't grind with its teeth, it smashed with its feet. It was different from the others, and it had horns on its head — ten of them. ⁸ Just as I was thinking about these horns, a smaller horn appeared, and three of the other horns were pulled

up by the roots to make room for it. This horn had the eyes of a human and a mouth that spoke with great pride.

[Daniel wrote:]

9   Thrones were set up
        while I was watching,
    and the Eternal God
        took his place.
    His clothing and his hair
        were white as snow.
    His throne was a blazing fire
        with fiery wheels,
10   and flames were dashing out
        from all around him.
    Countless thousands
    were standing there
        to serve him.
    The time of judgment began,
        and the books were opened.

11 I watched closely to see what would happen to this smaller horn because of the arrogant things it was saying. Then before my very eyes, the fourth beast was killed and its body destroyed by fire. 12 The other three beasts had their authority taken from them, but they were allowed to live a while longer. 13 As I continued to watch the vision that night,

    I saw what looked like
        a son of man
    coming with the clouds of heaven,
    and he was presented
        to the Eternal God.
14   He was crowned king
        and given power and glory,
    so that all people
    of every nation and race
        would serve him.
    He will rule forever,
    and his kingdom is eternal,
        never to be destroyed.

SEA READINGS ABOUT GOD'S ETERNAL REIGN

How the Apostles Mark, Luke and Paul Announced God's Eternal Reign

The first Christians, influenced by Daniel's visions, thought a lot about the end of the world. They were living in a very difficult time, much like today, when marching armies, proud empires and greedy merchants treated other people like dirty water. Not all of these Christians thought alike about the end-times. Some were more taken with Isaiah's view of a satisfying faithful life in this world, others with Daniel's vision of total chaos before God's final reign.

The gospel writer Mark and the apostle Paul, the two earliest New Testament writers, absorbed from Daniel's work the urgent need to proclaim what God was doing and the final promise of a heavenly reunion with God. Mark and Paul did not absorb into their view of God the grimness of Daniel's vision of war at the end of time. They believed that their Lord Jesus had already begun his eternal and authoritative reign when God sent his Son. Joy was already available for all who turned to God and were humbled through the message about Christ on the Cross. The exact time of the end was not for them to know. Mark and Paul did live around the Mediterranean Sea, so a peaceful sea was important to them, as it was in Daniel's vision. However, so too were clean rivers and a good supply of fish! Mark and Paul's belief was that the God who would bring about a heavenly reunion was also acting in the present creating and sustaining communities of faith, hope and love.

Mark 1.1-20
Good News About Jesus Christ

True North: The gospel writer Mark believed that the end times began when John the Baptizer announced Jesus would come to prepare God's way. John began the end times with lots of baptisms stirring up the river Jordan. Who could be solemn in a river of believers walking wet by God's action? Jesus affirmed the hope John had in him in his first sentence in this Gospel, "The time has come! God's kingdom will soon be here. Turn back to God and believe the good news!" Jesus' proclamation was not a call to convert to escape the wrath to come. It was an invitation to a promise already fulfilled. The good reign of God had already begun. Isn't it amazing that the first messengers of this joyful time called by Jesus were strong, responsible and cooperative fishers?

¹ This is the good news about Jesus Christ, the Son of God. ² It began just as God had said in the book written by Isaiah the prophet,
> "I am sending my messenger
>> to get the way ready
>> for you.
³ > In the desert
>> someone is shouting,
> 'Get the road ready
> for the Lord!
> Make a straight path
> for him.'"

⁴ So John the Baptist showed up in the desert and told everyone, "Turn back to God and be baptized! Then your sins will be forgiven." ⁵ From all Judea and Jerusalem crowds of people went to John. They told how sorry they were for their sins, and he baptized them in the Jordan River.
⁶ John wore clothes made of camel's hair. He had a leather strap around his waist and ate grasshoppers and wild honey.
⁷ John also told the people, "Someone more powerful is going to come. And I am not good enough even to stoop down and untie his sandals.
⁸ I baptize you with water, but he will baptize you with the Holy Spirit!"

⁹ About that time Jesus came from Nazareth in Galilee, and John baptized him in the Jordan River. ¹⁰ As soon as Jesus came out of the water, he saw the sky open and the Holy Spirit coming down to him like a dove. ¹¹ A voice from heaven said, "You are my own dear Son, and I am pleased with you."

¹² Right away God's Spirit made Jesus go into the desert. ¹³ He stayed there for forty days while Satan tested him. Jesus was with the wild animals, but angels took care of him.

¹⁴ After John was arrested, Jesus went to Galilee and told the good news that comes from God. ¹⁵ He said, "The time has come! God's kingdom will soon be here. d Turn back to God and believe the good news!"

¹⁶ As Jesus was walking along the shore of Lake Galilee, he saw Simon and his brother Andrew. They were fishermen and were casting their nets into the lake. ¹⁷ Jesus said to them, "Come with me! I will teach you how to bring in people instead of fish." ¹⁸ Right then the two brothers dropped their nets and went with him.

¹⁹ Jesus walked on and soon saw James and John, the sons of Zebedee. They were in a boat, mending their nets. ²⁰ At once Jesus asked them to come with him. They left their father in the boat with the hired workers and went with him.

Luke 21.25-28
Signs in the Heavens

True North: You know how important the signs in the sky are to seafarers. Luke prophesied about what these sky-signs meant. Changes in the sun, the moon, the stars and the sea foretold that God was bringing heaven's justice to bear on evil empires. God was saying, "Fear not, you will be set free." Believers took heart. How does this message comfort you? Read also the parallels in Matthew 24.29-31; Mark 13.24-26.

²⁵ Strange things will happen to the sun, moon, and stars. The nations on earth will be afraid of the roaring sea and tides, and they won't know what to do. ²⁶ People will be so frightened that they will faint because of what is happening to the world. Every power in the sky will be shaken. ²⁷ Then the Son of Man will be seen, coming in a

cloud with great power and glory. [28] When all of this starts happening, stand up straight and be brave. You will soon be set free.

1 Thessalonians 4.13–5.11
The Dead in Christ Shall Rise

True North: What an important concern the Thessalonians had! Will their Christian loved ones be raised when Christ comes from on high? Paul was so confident in his proclamation that Jesus was coming soon that it took everyone by surprise that some had died before Christ's return. Our grieving for those who have died in Christ is just as significant an experience as it was for the Thessalonians. The comfort for them and for us is that death cannot separate us from God since Christ has been raised. There is no need to be sorrowful (4.13) or get drunk (5.7). We are only temporarily apart from our loved ones. We shall meet the Lord in a glorious reunion. The dead in Christ shall rise before we who are alive!

How shall we live in light of this hope? Paul knew how. The news was so good about God's reconciliation to the world in Christ that everyone needed to be told about it, especially the neglected Gentiles. Yet, not all wanted to receive this good news. Some even persecuted Paul, Silvanus, Timothy and the Thessalonians. So, one must live then, as now, with faith, hope and love as our armor, polished and shining because of the good news! Paul did not believe there would be demonic beasts rising from the sea to wreak chaos on the world. Christ crucified and raised was chaos overcome. Encourage one another with these words (4.18).

[13] My friends, we want you to understand how it will be for those followers who have already died. Then you won't grieve over them and be like people who don't have any hope. [14] We believe that Jesus died and was raised to life. We also believe that when God brings Jesus back again, he will bring with him all who had faith in Jesus before they died. [15] Our Lord Jesus told us that when he comes, we won't go up to meet him ahead of his followers who have already died.

[16] With a loud command and with the shout of the chief angel and a blast of God's trumpet, the Lord will return from heaven. Then those who had faith in Christ before they died will be raised to life. [17]

Next, all of us who are still alive will be taken up into the clouds together with them to meet the Lord in the sky. From that time on we will all be with the Lord forever. [18] Encourage each other with these words.

5 [1] I don't need to write you about the time or date when all this will happen. [2] You surely know that the Lord's return will be as a thief coming at night. [3] People will think they are safe and secure. But destruction will suddenly strike them like the pains of a woman about to give birth. And they won't escape.

[4] My dear friends, you don't live in darkness, and so that day won't surprise you like a thief. [5] You belong to the light and live in the day. We don't live in the night or belong to the dark. [6] Others may sleep, but we should stay awake and be alert. [7] People sleep during the night, and some even get drunk. [8] But we belong to the day. So we must stay sober and let our faith and love be like a suit of armor. Our firm hope that we will be saved is our helmet.

[9] God doesn't intend to punish us, but wants us to be saved by our Lord Jesus Christ. [10] Christ died for us, so that we could live with him, whether we are alive or dead when he comes. [11] That's why you must encourage and help each other, just as you are already doing.

SEA READINGS ABOUT
GOD'S ETERNAL REIGN

How John of Patmos Received
A Vision of God's Eternal Reign

John of Patmos had read the Scriptures many times before he had his revelation and wrote it down. His vision combined many of the images of the waters of chaos and the waters of life that you have read about in WaterWords. John's revelation was that at the end of time there would be a final reconciliation of the tension between the salty wild waters and the fresh calm waters. He saw also that God would finally overthrow the evil seafaring merchant nations.

In the Old Testament, Babylon and Tyre were the names of two real cities that almost destroyed God's people. In John's Revelation, the "new Babylon" and the "new Tyre" was Rome, with its beast-like emperors and armies arising from the sea. Yet John never named Rome directly since he worried about Christians being persecuted. His first readers would have easily understood his hidden references to Rome and his number symbolism. We do not understand so easily, although we do know that the number seven (7) in the texts is the number of heavenly perfection.

John left open to us the option of understanding his prophecy in any context where people are so oppressed by armies and naval forces that they cannot imagine that they can do anything about it. In John's vision, this situation would prevail at the end of time. Only God could overcome chaos with order. John's vision was that the agent for this change was Jesus Christ. He would lead the heavenly armies as the Lamb of God and would reign forever. For John, the end time would be soon.

We know that God did act. The empire of Rome did fall. That beast is no more. But it didn't prove to be the end of time. Our lives still go on. So each of us must consider which vision of prophecy makes sense to us. What do you think the eternal reign of God will be like? And where and when will it occur? On earth or in heaven?

Revelation 5.11-14; 14.6-7
Praise and Repentance

True North: *The vision John received showed that the earth would be close to an end when everyone worshiped God through praise and repentance. John's vision reminded his Christian friends to be faithful to God now. How about you?*

[11] As I looked, I heard the voices of a lot of angels around the throne and the voices of the living creatures and of the elders. There were millions and millions of them, [12] and they were saying in a loud voice,
"The Lamb who was killed
is worthy to receive power,
riches, wisdom, strength,
honor, glory, praise."
[13] Then I heard all beings in heaven and on the earth and under the earth and in the sea offer praise. Together, all of them were saying,
"Praise, honor, glory,
and strength
forever and ever
to the one who sits
on the throne
and to the Lamb!"
[14] The four living creatures said "Amen," while the elders knelt down and worshiped.

14 [6] I saw another angel. This one was flying across the sky and had the eternal good news to announce to the people of every race, tribe, language, and nation on earth. [7] The angel shouted, "Worship and honor God! The time has come for him to judge everyone. Kneel down before the one who created heaven and earth, the oceans, and every stream."

Revelation 10.1-7
Promises of Salvation

True North: John of Patmos' vision was that at the end of time there would be no more delay in the judgment of evil empires which led people astray.

10 I saw another powerful angel come down from heaven. This one was covered with a cloud, and a rainbow was over his head. His face was like the sun, his legs were like columns of fire, [2] and with his hand he held a little scroll that had been unrolled. He stood there with his right foot on the sea and his left foot on the land. [3] Then he shouted with a voice that sounded like a growling lion. Thunder roared seven times.

[4] After the thunder stopped, I was about to write what it had said. But a voice from heaven shouted, "Keep it secret! Don't write these things."

[5] The angel I had seen standing on the sea and the land then held his right hand up toward heaven. [6] He made a promise in the name of God who lives forever and who created heaven, earth, the sea, and every living creature. The angel said, "You won't have to wait any longer. [7] God told his secret plans to his servants the prophets, and it will all happen by the time the seventh angel sounds his trumpet."

Revelation 15.1-4
Life's Precious Waters
Now Flow From God's Throne

True North: Water is necessary for life. The rivers of life first flowed in the Garden of Eden with their sweet water. John saw that they would flow again at the end of time. The sea would become solid glass and would no longer take its toll on seafarers. The song believers would sing when the sea became solid would be like Moses' and Miriam's song of victory after God parted the Red Sea (Ex 15.1-21). Thank God for this coming victory!

15 After this, I looked at the sky and saw something else that was strange and important. Seven angels were bringing the last seven terrible troubles. When these are ended, God will no longer be angry.

² Then I saw something that looked like a glass sea mixed with fire, and people were standing on it. They were the ones who had defeated the beast and the idol and the number that tells the name of the beast. God had given them harps, ³ and they were singing the song that his servant Moses and the Lamb had sung. They were singing,

> "Lord God All-Powerful,
> you have done great
>   and marvelous things.
> You are the ruler
>   of all nations,
> and you do what is
>   right and fair.
> ⁴ Lord, who doesn't honor
>   and praise your name?
> You alone are holy,
> and all nations will come
>   and worship you,
> because you have shown
> that you judge
>   with fairness."

Revelation 17.1-5
If Only There Had Been a
Seafarers' Center in Babylon!

True North: John of Patmos believed, as the prophet Isaiah did, that port cities prostituted themselves. In his vision the beast with seven heads represented these port cities and empires who pretended to be holy and fooled people. As a seafarer, you know which cities make prostitutes of themselves. They make you feel very far from home and then prey on your loneliness and cabin fever. Does coming into port worry you when you have been so long at sea? You know that in the harbors of such cities, there is danger to yourself from unjust ship owners and uncaring immigration agents as well as from prostitutes and thieves. This is why Bethel chapels were established in England two centuries ago. They were founded to be safe, clean, well-lighted places for companionship, bible study, good food, recreation and prayer with caring believers. At seafarers' centers your money won't be taken unlawfully, and you will not endanger your life through disease. Jesus has asked us to do this for you.

17 One of the seven angels who had emptied the bowls came over and said to me, "Come on! I will show you how God will punish that shameless prostitute who sits on many oceans. ² Every king on earth has slept with her, and her shameless ways are like wine that has made everyone on earth drunk."

³ With the help of the Spirit, the angel took me into the desert, where I saw a woman sitting on a red beast. The beast was covered with names that were an insult to God, and it had seven heads and ten horns. ⁴ The woman was dressed in purple and scarlet robes, and she wore jewelry made of gold, precious stones, and pearls. In her hand she held a gold cup filled with the filthy and nasty things she had done. ⁵ On her forehead a mysterious name was written:

I AM THE GREAT CITY OF BABYLON,
THE MOTHER OF EVERY IMMORAL
AND FILTHY THING ON EARTH.

Revelation 18.1-3, 15-22
John's Prophecy:
At the End of Time, God Will Destroy
the Most Evil Seafaring Empire That John Could Imagine

True North: *John of Patmos used the images of Babylon from Ezekiel 27.1-36 as the background for this prophecy about Rome. What city or nation do you think fits this description? Pray that it will be raised up from wickedness to justice. Pray that you might be safe there. Pray that you might be a witness to a more holy and just way for people to act when you visit there.*

18 I saw another angel come from heaven. This one had great power, and the earth was bright because of his glory. ² The angel shouted,
> "Fallen! Powerful Babylon
>> has fallen
> and is now the home
>> of demons.
> It is the den
>> of every filthy spirit
> and of all unclean birds,
> and every dirty
>> and hated animal.
> ³ Babylon's evil and immoral wine
>> has made all nations drunk.
> Every king on earth
>> has slept with her,
> and every merchant on earth
> is rich because of
>> her evil desires."

¹⁵ The merchants had become rich because of her. But when they saw her sufferings, they were terrified. They stood at a distance, crying and mourning. ¹⁶ Then they shouted,

"Pity the great city
of Babylon!
She dressed in fine linen
and wore purple
and scarlet cloth.
She had jewelry
made of gold
and precious stones
and pearls.
¹⁷ Yet in a single hour
her riches disappeared."

Every ship captain and passenger and sailor stood at a distance, together with everyone who does business by traveling on the sea. ¹⁸ When they saw the smoke from her fire, they shouted, "This was the greatest city ever!"

¹⁹ They cried loudly, and in their sorrow they threw dust on their heads, as they said,

"Pity the great city
of Babylon!
Everyone who sailed the seas
became rich
from her treasures.
But in a single hour
the city was destroyed.
²⁰ The heavens should be happy
with God's people
and apostles and prophets.
God has punished her
for them."

²¹ A powerful angel then picked up a huge stone and threw it into the sea. The angel said,

"This is how the great city
of Babylon
will be thrown down,
never to rise again.

22 The music of harps and singers
and of flutes and trumpets
    will no longer be heard.
No workers will ever
    set up shop in that city,
and the sound
of grinding grain
    will be silenced forever.

Revelation 20.1-3, 11-15
The Sea Gave Up Its Dead
And the Sea and Death Were No More.

True North: *John saw that at the end of time the sea dragon Leviathan would be locked away. John knew this sea monster had the same desires for chaos and evil that the snake Satan did when our first parents sinned (Gn 3.1-24). At the end of time, God would make the sea give back the bodies of drowned seafarers from its kingdom of the dead below the waters. John of Patmos saw that after all were judged, it would be death and the kingdom of death which would be sent into a lake of fire. Praise God!*

20 I saw an angel come down from heaven, carrying the key to the deep pit and a big chain. ² He chained the dragon for a thousand years. It is that old snake, who is also known as the devil and Satan. ³ Then the angel threw the dragon into the pit. He locked and sealed it, so that a thousand years would go by before the dragon could fool the nations again. But after that, it would have to be set free for a little while.

¹¹ I saw a great white throne with someone sitting on it. Earth and heaven tried to run away, but there was no place for them to go. ¹² I also saw all the dead people standing in front of that throne. Every one of them was there, no matter who they had once been. Several books were opened, and then the book of life was opened. The dead were judged by what those books said they had done.

¹³ The sea gave up the dead people who were in it, and death and its kingdom also gave up their dead. Then everyone was judged by what they had done. ¹⁴ Afterwards, death and its kingdom were thrown into the lake of fire. This is the second death. ¹⁵ Anyone whose name wasn't written in the book of life was thrown into the lake of fire.

Revelation 21.1-8
No More Tears!
God's Home is With God's People

True North: John of Patmos saw that God would dwell among us at the end of time, but not on earth as we know it. God would create a new holy city and a new heaven and earth. In that new city there would be no pain, mourning or crying. The sea would be violent no more. There would be no more hard labor to take you away from your families for so long. Comfort yourself and your loved ones with these words. And praise God for wanting to love us until the end of time.

21 I saw a new heaven and a new earth. The first heaven and the first earth had disappeared, and so had the sea. ² Then I saw New Jerusalem, that holy city, coming down from God in heaven. It was like a bride dressed in her wedding gown and ready to meet her husband.

³ I heard a loud voice shout from the throne:

God's home is now with his people. He will live with them, and they will be his own. Yes, God will make his home among his people. ⁴ He will wipe all tears from their eyes, and there will be no more death, suffering, crying, or pain. These things of the past are gone forever.

⁵ Then the one sitting on the throne said:

I am making everything new. Write down what I have said. My words are true and can be trusted. ⁶ Everything is finished! I am Alpha and Omega, the beginning and the end. I will freely give water from the life-giving fountain to everyone who is thirsty. ⁷ All who win the victory will be given these blessings. I will be their God, and they will be my people.

⁸ But I will tell you what will happen to cowards and to everyone who is unfaithful or dirty-minded or who murders or is sexually immoral or uses witchcraft or worships idols or tells lies. They will be thrown into that lake of fire and burning sulfur. This is the second death.

Revelation 22.1-5, 16-17
Life-giving Water for Free!

True North: John's vision concluded happily after he saw that all would be light and life in the new Jerusalem which had now come down to earth. All human thirsts would be quenched and all needs met just as Isaiah had prophesied (Is. 55.1). The trees of the Garden of Eden, including the Tree of Life, had been forbidden to people after our first parents sinned (Gn. 2.4-3.24). Now believers would be able to eat of their fruit and the nations would be healed by their leaves.

What John of Patmos saw in a vision did occur in part. We know that God did act and the empire of Rome did fall. That beast that rose at the edge of the sea to harm others and grasp for power was no more. However, the end of Rome did not prove to be the end of time. Our lives still go on. So each of you, as seafarers, must consider which prophecy, proclamation or vision about the future completion of God's reign makes the most sense to you. You may find yourself thinking a lot about your choice, since each view of the end time has behind it a view of how God has worked in the past and how God is working now in you. You have many prophecies, proclamations, and visions to consider, since we have looked at the views of Isaiah, Ezekiel, Daniel, Mark, Luke, Paul and John of Patmos. What do you think the eternal reign of God will be like? Where and when will it occur? On earth or in heaven? Thanks be to God that God's action is not dependent on our decision! God has acted for us in Christ and Christ will assure our salvation at the end-time whatever that end-time might be!

While all these witnesses to the end of time that you have read about in WaterWords did not agree on whether the beginning of God's final kind reign would occur on earth or in heaven, they did all agree on this about God's eternal reign. Living water, peaceful water, sweet water comes from God. We agree and say to you, "Come all you seafarers and fishers! If you want life-giving water, come and take it! It's free!"

22 The angel showed me a river that was crystal clear, and its waters gave life. The river came from the throne where God and the Lamb were seated. ² Then it flowed down the middle of the city's main street. On each side of the river are trees that grow a different kind of fruit each month of the year. The fruit gives life, and the leaves are used as medicine to heal the nations.

³ God's curse will no longer be on the people of that city. He and the Lamb will be seated there on their thrones, and its people will worship God ⁴ and will see him face to face. God's name will be written on the foreheads of the people. ⁵ Never again will night appear, and no one who lives there will ever need a lamp or the sun. The Lord God will be their light, and they will rule forever.

¹⁶ I am Jesus! And I am the one who sent my angel to tell all of you these things for the churches. I am David's Great Descendant, and I am also the bright morning star.

¹⁷ The Spirit and the bride say, "Come!"

Everyone who hears this should say, "Come!"

If you are thirsty, come! If you want life-giving water, come and take it. It's free!

WaterWords
Index of Readings

Old Testament

Old Testament Apocrypha

New Testament

New from ...

MARITIME LIBRARY

COMPANION TO WATERWORDS BY DR. ROBIN DALE MATTISON

ISBN 0-9673673-5-2   US$5.95 each

A perfect companion to *WaterWords*, this journal helps you to make the most out of your *WaterWords* reflections. Written by Dr. Robin Mattison, the author of *WaterWords*, it provides expanded journaling help as well as ample space to write your own reflections. The journal is designed with your practical use in mind in a convenient 8.5X5.5 inch format bound with durable spiral binding that opens and lays flat for writing. The cover is laminated with plastic for durability and protection.

To order your copy visit www.mallpublishing.com, send e-mail to info@mallpublishing.com or write to Customer Service, Mall Publishing, Inc., 10240 W. Ames Ave., Beach Park IL 60099 USA.

A Maritime Library Exclusive

MARITIME ART OF YONG XIAN-RANG

Former Head of Folk Art Department at the Central Academy of Art in Beijing, Professor Yong Xian-rang has gained international recognition for his impressive facility and flexibility in painting and printmaking. His works of art are treasured in collections in Britain, Japan, France, Korea, Taiwan and the United States. His art, specially dedicated to the *People of the Sea* is featured on the cover of this book.

Maritime Library is proud to present his full color paintings in limited edition lithographs, on note cards, post cards and on bulletin or program blanks.

Additionally a full complement of creative resources for Maritime Ministry are available from Maritime Library.

For information or for orders visit www.mallpublishing.com or email info@mallpublishing. Our mailing address is 10240 W Ames Av., Beach Park IL 60099 USA.